AF333623

Love Before the Fall

Love Before the Fall

by

WILLIAM D. DEAN

THE WESTMINSTER PRESS

Philadelphia

Book Design by Dorothy Alden Smith

Published by The Westminster Press®
Philadelphia, Pennsylvania

PRINTED IN THE UNITED STATES OF AMERICA

Library of Congress Cataloging in Publication Data

Dean, William D
Love before the fall.

Includes bibliographical references.
1. Love—Addresses, essays, lectures. I. Title
BD436.D4   128′.3   75–42226
ISBN 0–664–24792–X

To my parents and to my children,
who give lessons in love

CONTENTS

PREFACE

The following lectures were delivered silently in my office, by a pencil to blank sheets of paper.

They are an excerpt from a noisy dialogue with absent companions, some of them theologians, some philosophers, some writers, and most of them dead.

The following lectures have sought in solitude to describe through dialogue what it is that overcomes solitude.

The lectures are lectures on love. The word "love" refers to many diverse phenomena; and among those are two phenomena which these lectures discuss. Sometimes love refers to the fact that people are together, rather than apart from each other; and these lectures seek to say how people overcome solitude in order to be together. Sometimes love refers to an experience that is satisfying simply to experience; and these lectures seek to say how social togetherness is a satisfaction to experience. To emphasize the satisfaction in the experience of social togetherness we have designated the love discussed in these lectures as "aesthetic love."

Why aesthetic love is an appropriate designation can be explained through the use of two metaphors: "after the fall" and "before the fall." Life after the fall of humankind is the life preoccupied with human failure and the means for overcoming it. Life before the fall, used metaphorically, does not refer to a prehistoric time, but to a quality of present life. It refers to those infrequent moments when the struggle against failure is not paramount, and when the appreciation of present moments is appropriate. In the first metaphor, love is an ethical act; love must strive, as moral acts do, to be a means for the eventual improvement of life. In the second metaphor, love is an aesthetic act; love seeks, as aesthetic pursuits do, to be an inherently valuable event, which is satisfying simply to experience. In these lectures we will seek to define, to explain, and to advocate this love before the fall, this aesthetic love.

The lectures that follow were shaped, consciously and unconsciously, by the ideas and concerns peculiarly germane to academic theology. Also, the lectures were a response, knowingly and unknowingly, to the allure and the confusion which seems to underlie practical religion wherever it exists. The lectures are, very obliquely, a proposal in sympathy with the theologically neglected New Testament idea of *koinonia,* or fellowship. These lectures are lectures about an aesthetic love which is a religious love. Even God enters the picture.

Finally, two retrospective comments are in order. First, in one respect in particular these lectures are incomplete; they have omitted consideration of the other aspect of the life before the fall. That life has, in addition to the social dimension, the individual dimension. However, this omission is intentional; my previous book, *Coming To: A Theology of Beauty,* is an effort to discuss the aesthetic experience of the solitary individual.

Second, I am indebted to those who helped me with this book. I am indebted to my colleagues, Richard Fuller and John Rezmerski, for their criticism and their encouragement. I am indebted to Nancy Benjamin, my secretary, and to Lorraine Anderson, who typed the manuscript. And, most of all, I am indebted to Patricia Dean, who among other things is my wife, and who with exhausting rigor and logic and sensitivity and imagination did what humanly could be done to get me to think better and to write better.

I:
Common Sense and Aesthetic Love

Ladies and Gentlemen:

I will speak about love this evening, and for the four evenings that follow.

Let me begin by telling you about Plato and Jesus. For them, love occurs after paradise is lost. Love, for them, has no apparent connection with the good life, the life before paradise is lost. Plato's and Jesus' heads were filled with the reverberations from humanity's great fall from paradise. Love came only after that fall, to silence the sinful and mortal clamor. Love was to confront what had gone wrong, to overcome it, and to return humanity to its primal and proper tranquillity. But, regarding that primal tranquillity, regarding the state of life or love before the fall, Jesus and Plato are quite silent.

A view of life requires some view of ideal human contact, or love. The life after the fall, permeated as it is by human failure, requires a corrective love. But the life before the fall conjures up the literalist's picture of "how it was in Eden" or the modernist's aspiration for the good life now. The question Jesus and Plato leave unanswered is, What is the life before the fall, and what love does it require?

Love in the Bible occurs after the fall, after the disobedience in the Garden of Eden, after the consequent "wickedness, evil, covetousness, and malice" arose in people's hearts. Love was to overcome these failings. Love was to heal the sickness, to right the wrongs incurred in the fall. Love in the Bible aimed, finally, to restore humanity to its original condition. But, about love in the life that might have been before the fall, the Bible is silent.

Jesus was probably not interested in that question. For Jesus the first paradise, the Garden of Eden, would be restored in the future paradise, the Kingdom of God. But what love might be in either paradise, was a question that seemed to need no answer.

It was as though the paradisal life itself, the life before the fall, was obvious and nonproblematic. So Jesus could concentrate on what was unknown and problematic: how to overcome sin, to negate the negative, to return to zero, to the even point between the negative life after the fall and the positive life before the fall. It was assumed that the positive life, including a positive love, was known. The recovery of that life was the final reason for our present struggles. However, for many of us the life and love before the fall are not at all obvious.

Neither did Plato bother to tell us of a love before the fall. Plato tells of a soul who, in her travels around the region of heaven, "meeting with some mischance comes to be burdened with a load of forgetfulness and wrongdoing, and because of that burden sheds her wings and falls to the earth."[1] Love comes after this fall and seeks to overcome this forgetfulness by eliciting insight from the beloved. This insight fosters the recollection which restores one to one's natural state of enlightenment. But as to what love might have been before enlightenment was lost or might be after enlightenment is attained, Plato is silent. If that love is obvious to Plato, it is not so to many of us.

Did Plato assume that we already knew what that primal life, with its primal love, might be? Clearly, the recovery of that life is meant to be the final cause for one's present strivings. But without knowledge of that life and that love, we have no final cause for the love Plato advocates, we have no end for that means.

Jesus' love, often called *agape*, and Plato's love, often called *eros*, are painful struggles to deal with loss. Theoretically, when the loss is overcome, when the need is resolved, *agape* and *eros* are defunct. Then, presumably, having struggled up the stairs, humanity will proceed with that life, the recovery of which motivated the preceding struggles.

But what if we do not know about paradise? What if we really do not know of the life before the fall? What if we have long since lost any belief in a literal Garden of Eden or Kingdom of God or mythical heaven of the immortals?

Many of us, instead of knowing the positive life and its love, have become those who know the negative life, the life of struggle. We may no longer yearn for a paradise beyond history but hope merely for fragmentary blessings in present history.

We need knowledge of love before the fall, rather than of love after the fall. We are inclined to say that, without some present prospect of experiencing, at least fleetingly, love in the good life, now, love after the fall is not worth the struggle.

What if we are not willing to climb the stairs or help

our friends climb the stairs, if there are not occasional days, hours or minutes when the door is opened and we can go inside?

The fall of humanity, its heavy involvement in perversity, is obvious. *Agape* and *eros,* as efforts to deal with the sin and blindness caused by human failure, are necessary. The problem is not to convince people of the fall and the need for the struggle against it. The problem is to say what prevents a complete preoccupation with the fall.

The problem is to identify a love for before the fall but possible in present existence.

We will attempt to meet that problem by proposing a love appropriate to the time before the fall. We will call this love aesthetic love because it is a love that functions as aesthetic phenomena do; it is an inherently valuable event that is satisfying simply to experience. We will contrast this love with *agape* and *eros,* which are ethical loves because they function as morality does, as a means to a better future.

This proposal of an aesthetic love will be validated not by the venerable authorities, such as Jesus or Plato, nor by the modern scientific methodologies; rather, this proposal will be placed before the timeless bar of common understanding, or common sense. The appeal to common sense will function as the final arbiter of the validity of a notion of aesthetic love. This is to assume that common sense has implicit in it an empirical side and an ideal side, and that common sense can identify certain empirical phenomena as examples of ideal types. In this lecture common sense will identify phenomena as examples of particular ideal types of love. This use of common sense is, formally at least, in tune with Jesus and Plato; Jesus' sermons and Plato's dialogues appealed to common people for confirmation. Jesus thought his followers could understand his sermons because the followers were children of Israel and had within them the image of God. Plato thought people could recognize truth in events around them because they could recollect the truth from a heavenly preexistence. We will follow Jesus and Plato, then, in an appeal to common sense.

Also, we will follow Jesus and Plato to their conclusion that it is impossible to explain love without mentioning God or some ultimate reality.

Prior to our appeal to common sense, we must comment on Jesus' *agape* and Plato's *eros*. Then, very abstractly, we will propose a definition of aesthetic love.

Agape is a Greek word which is translated "love" in English translations of the New Testament. The verb *agapan* occurs 141 times in the New Testament and the noun *agape* occurs 116 times. No other Greek word is so often translated "love" in English translations of the New Testament. The next most frequent Greek word occurs as the verb *philein* ("to love, like") 25 times and as the noun *philos* ("friend") 29 times.[2] The Greek word *eros* is not used in the New Testament. So it is not surprising that scholars call the New Testament notion of love *agape*.

They go on to say that the distinctiveness of *agape* is most apparent in the following instances: in Jesus' admonition that one should love one's enemies, in the parables of the good Samaritan and the prodigal son, and in the crucifixion. In each of these instances the one who is loved is not particularly lovable or valuable for the one doing the loving. So *agape* is a love that is said not to be caused, or elicited, by the lovableness or value of the beloved. The beloved is not only not lovable or valuable; the beloved is thought of as one without some particular value and with some particular need for a value. On the other hand, the lover is thought to possess whatever value it is that will meet the need of the beloved. However, in the New Testament the lover is not autonomous. The value the *agape* lover gives is instilled in the lover by a God who first loved the lover; many theologians say that the ultimate cause of *agape* is God, while the proximate cause is the lover. In *agape*, then, something is given, or imparted, by the lover to the beloved, whether that be succor or salvation.

Eros is the Greek word that is translated "love" in the English translations of the writings of Plato. Scholars of the classics apparently refrain from word counts, at least to the extent indulged in by scholars of the New Testament, so we cannot report how many times *eros* occurs in Plato, either in verbal or nominal form.

Plato's talk of *eros* is permeated with talk of sex; it is apparent that sex, at least as an analogy, is deemed instructive. In the *Phaedrus*, Plato says that the lover, before being brought under control, goes for the beloved, "after the fashion of a four-footed beast, and to beget offspring of the flesh,"[3] or like an unruly steed, dragging the charioteer and a second horse after him, in mad charge after the beloved.[4] And in the *Symposium* the ascent of love toward more and more noble objects of loving attention begins with the love of a body, whether that be the body of a woman or of a boy.[5] It is, in short, the beauty of the beloved's body which initially attracts the lover.

The beautiful is attractive because it inspires in the

one who beholds it the desire for possession; when the lover beholds the beautiful, the lover wants to possess the beautiful. This desire grows more sophisticated, so the lover's quest proceeds on an ascending scale to more universal and essential beauty, until there is attained the vision of beauty itself, free from any mortal impediment.

Plato's notion of *eros* is virtually the converse of *agape. Eros* is a love stimulated by the value of the beloved. In *eros* the dynamic is not that of giving, but of receiving or, possibly, of taking—by the lover from the beloved. It is the lover who is in need, and the beloved who has available, to yield to the lover, what the lover needs. However, the beloved is not an autonomous source of value. The ultimate source of the beloved's value is the idea of beauty itself, or absolute beauty. Assuming a didactic stance, Socrates says to Agathon, "one, that Love is always the love of something, and two, that that something is what he lacks."[6]

In the Western world Jesus and Plato provide the two seminal expressions of love after the fall, and they have overshadowed all other Western comment on love. In the twentieth century, Anders Nygren initiated the modern discussion of these forms of love[7] in a book appropriately entitled *Agape and Eros.* For Nygren the essential difference between *agape* and *eros* is that, while *agape* is indifferent to the value of the beloved, *eros* seeks to acquire the value of the beloved for one's self. Nygren argues that both Christian *agape* and Greek *eros* are empowered, finally, not by the parties to the loves, but by God or some supernatural reality.

There is, then, one spectrum, with *agape* at one end and *eros* at the other. Most contemporary theories of love can be placed somewhere on that spectrum. Most Christian theories of love range from the midpoint, the point where Augustine's notion of love might be located, to the *agape* end. Numerous secular theories of love would fall at the *eros* end of the spectrum. Rather arbitrarily we could name a couple. Novelist Henry Miller seems to follow Plato, even to the extent of desiring mystical contact with absolute beauty itself.[8] Comparative psychologist Harry Harlow, in *Learning to Love*,[9] describes five forms of love in rhesus monkeys: (1) maternal love; (2) infant love, the love of the infant for the mother; (3) peer love, the love of child for child; (4) heterosexual love; (5) parental love, or the love of the adult male for his family or his social group. Harlow, with an odd disrespect for complexity, is not at all reluctant to apply his findings more or less wholesale to humans, or to intersperse comments on rhesus monkeys with comments on humans so indiscriminately that often the reader is unaware of the species of Harlow's referent. But his picture of love is a picture of erotic love: in all five forms of love the basic impetus to love is the lover's desire for the comfort provided by contact with the beloved.

All loves on the spectrum from *agape* to *eros* are loves for after the fall. A problem, expressed as a need, is assumed, and love is a transaction whereby value is transferred from one who has value to one who needs value. Not surprisingly a love for before the fall, a love not primarily concerned with overcoming deficits, does not fit on this spectrum. This love, aesthetic love, is a noncausal, nontemporal and nonindividualistic love. However, rather than speak so negatively about aesthetic love, it may be best to define aesthetic love by showing how it is opposed to *agape* and *eros*. Let me list the opposing features in terms of three categories, which provide the basis for a distinction between two basic models, or paradigms, of love.

1. *Causality. Agape* and *eros* interpret human relations in terms of causality. The agapic lover is the proximate cause, transmitting a gift of value to the beloved, who receives the effect of the lover's giving. The erotic lover is the proximate cause, taking or acquiring the value the beloved has. On the other hand, aesthetic love interprets human relations in a noncausal way. Aesthetic love is a noncausal bond among parties to the love.[10]

2. *Temporality. Agape* and *eros*, like all causal actions, occur through moments of time; from their causal action to their effects, they extend through time. The agapic lover gives in one moment of time and the beloved receives the gift in a later moment of time. The erotic lover solicits the beloved's value, the beloved imparts value, and the lover receives that value, each at successively later moments of time. Aesthetic love, on the other hand, transpires in the present moment, among contemporaries.

3. *Individuality. Agape* and *eros* pertain to individuals. These loves pertain to how a lover acts, while alone in the present, actual moment, while literally separated from the beloved, who is known as he or she was in an earlier moment of time. Aesthetic love pertains to a social relatedness among people in the present, actual world.

These three differences align *agape* and *eros* with ethics, and aesthetic love with aesthetics.

Agape and *eros* aim toward a realization of value in the future, extrinsic to the lover's present. The *agape* lover acts causally, as an individual, to transmit value to meet the beloved's need. The *eros* lover acts causally, as an individual, to implement the eventual transmittal of value from the beloved to meet the lover's own need. The causal, temporal, and individualistic natures of *agape* and *eros* mean that they serve extrinsic values, values extrinsic to the lover's present. As a consequence, *agape* and *eros* are ethical loves, because ethics pertains to actions not normally considered to be intrinsically valuable, but extrinsically valuable, as a means for the attainment of some future benefit. There are two modern ways of speaking about ethics. The first, instrumentalism, or utilitarianism, because it argues that the pursuit of future ends justifies present means, clearly conforms to the pursuit of what is extrinsically valuable. The second, deontological, legalistic, or duty ethics, claims to be concerned exclusively with the purity of the means alone. However, a closer analysis reveals that this ethical approach finally requires attention to consequences, and is in some major way concerned with extrinsic value.[11] It is because of this correlation with ethics that we are calling *agape* and *eros* ethical loves.

Aesthetic love, because it is noncausal, nontemporal and nonindividual, belongs to the realm of aesthetics. Aesthetic love is socially actualized in the noncausal, nontemporal present. Consequently, the phenomena of aesthetic love, like the phenomena of aesthetic experience, are intrinsic to one's own present; both are inherently, or intrinsically, valuable for the self. It is because of this correlation with aesthetics that we are calling the love before the fall an aesthetic love.

Of course, these abstract comments do violence to the subtle and evanescent experience of love itself. So the comments should be seen as no more than distant and pale reflections of the realities of love. They are no more than a beginning to any description of love.

Through the remainder of this lecture we will provide a more concrete, a more empirical, description of *agape, eros,* and aesthetic love. These descriptions will take the form of illustrations about three areas of human experience: sexual relations, race relations, and education. The illustrations should demonstrate, first, that our abstract comments on love apply to concrete experience and, second, that common sense can identify these experiences as examples of various ideal types of love.

1. *Sexual Relations.* Illustrations about sex are always controversial, but in the era of women's liberation they may be even politically controversial. To be specific, our illustrations about agapic and erotic sex are offensive. The question is, why are they offensive? Our suggestion is that they are offensive because we have in our common sense a third ideal about sex, and it is from the standpoint of this ideal that agapic and erotic sex are offensive.

Agape and *eros,* as forms of sexual love, are best described as acts of seduction. As terms in the metaphor of seduction, *agape* is exercised by the seducee, usually the stereotypical female, and *eros* is exercised by the seducer, usually the stereotypical male.

The *agape* lover is the shrinking violet, offering herself for seduction. With Christian compassion for her beloved, she gives her value to meet his needs. As Nygren would say, her act is motivated by no interest whatsoever in his value. As Reinhold Niebuhr would say, her act is self-sacrificial.

The *eros* lover is the seducer. With Greek passion he takes his beloved's value to resolve his need. As Nygren would say, his act is egocentrically concerned for the acquisition of her value for himself. As Niebuhr would say, his lust for power is limitless and destructive if left unchecked and unbalanced by a self-interested demand on her part.

The *agape* lover's giving does not depend solely on her possession of much value and no need. It depends also on the recognition that her beloved has much need and no value, and that she must impart her value to meet his need. And his taking does not depend solely on his possession of much need and no value. It depends also on the recognition that she has much value and no need, and that, eventually, she should yield to his need by imparting her value. But the key to it all is that through time one who is sexually indifferent (has no need) must, through evidence of her partner's need, be persuaded to act. That project is called seduction.

But the seduction must never be consummated. If the transaction of her value to meet his need were ever to be completed, the love would cease. How could she give, agapically, to one whose need is already fulfilled? How could he desire, erotically, that which he already has? When boy gets girl, the drama is over. The house lights go up. For those who want the seduction to go on, at least in the mind, there must be no happy resolution.

There must be separation or the introduction of an insurmountable obstacle to sexual consummation. The procedures of seduction require deprivation. If deprivation is overcome, seduction is irrelevant.

So long as deprivation is sustained, and so long as both lovers know that, then the *eros* lover and the *agape* lover each perform rather individual and isolated functions. They are like gyroscopes, guided by an orientation that is utterly internal. She has her gift and her motion is giving; he has his need and his motion is taking. They bump, and keep spinning at the selfsame tilt. And in the bump there is no community.

Aesthetic lovers, on the other hand, perform socially. They approach each other with a problem that must be described socially: they are apart and they ought to be together. The need for sex does not refer to one individual's problem; the value in sex does not refer to one individual's value. The problem is isolation where there should be commune; the value lies in the social contact, not in either individual. Sexual consummation, then, is a proper conclusion for sex according to the model of aesthetic love.

In aesthetic love, sexual contact is concerned primarily with intrinsic value. To speak of sexual contact without primary emphasis on present satisfaction is to miss the point. Seduction would miss the point. Seduction can be maintained only with present deprivation, not present satisfaction. The intrinsic value of sex can be appreciated only when it subscribes to the model of aesthetic love, when sexual love is a noncausal relationship existing in the present moment of time and experienced with immediate satisfaction.

The value of this relationship concerns not the transaction of a quantity of value through time, but the quality of the relationship in the present moment of time. This quality is best described aesthetically.

This entire illustration of sexual relations may seem to put *agape* and *eros* in an unfavorable light. It takes little imagination to see that *agape* and *eros* are so dissimilar that they oppose each other like pieces in a puzzle, and to see that, with a little extrapolation, *agape* and *eros* provide a perfect rationale for sadomasochistic sex. But such extrapolation does not necessarily follow. We mean to say only that ideal sexual practice cannot be described in terms of either *agape* or *eros*, and we mean to suggest that ideal sexual relations can be described in terms of aesthetic love. That this is true can be confirmed by an appeal to common sense—as well as to most contemporary sex manuals.

2. *Race Relations.* When in the United States *agape* was practiced by the whites to help the blacks, sometimes very good things happened. Sometimes real needs were appropriately met. White liberals, for example, did help to bring about the passage of federal desegregation and voting rights laws in the 1950's and the 1960's, and these were beneficial to the blacks.

Similarly, there is something salubrious in the new appreciation of black culture in the United States. There is a proper *eros,* by white culture, for the distinctive creativity of the black culture.

However, there is another practice in the racial situation in the United States which is valuable. It has to do neither with an agapic exchange of value, from white lover to black beloved, nor an erotic exchange of value, from black beloved to white lover. It has to do with a social solidarity between whites and blacks; this solidarity is sometimes referred to by the term, "integration." The value in this social condition resides in the "being together" of whites and blacks; it resides in their being as one people, in the present moment of time. Integration so conceived is a diversity of people living, at least temporarily, in conjunction. The experience of this diversity in conjunction can be a pleasure; it can be an aesthetic experience. This experience can and does occur in interracial gatherings of all sorts.

This experience of integration is an experience of aesthetic love. This aesthetic love is not an individual, but a social reality; it resolves the need implicit in isolation—in this case, the isolation of one group from another group. Integration is not merely the absence of the condition of isolation, however, just as genuine peace is not merely the absence of war. Integration is a positive social reality that has a positive quality— diversity in conjunction.

The *agape* and the *eros* of the white for the black do not refer to a valuable social reality between the races. They refer to a causal exchange of values between individual groups isolated from each other in different moments of time. There are two temporal phases in *agape:* first, the white lover gives value; then, a moment later, the black beloved receives that value. There are four temporal phases in *eros:* first, the white lover solicits the black's value; second, the black receives that solicitation; third, the black relinquishes value; and fourth, the white receives that value. The white and the black are isolated from each other in earlier and later moments of time. Individual needs may be met by the exchange of values, but there is no social reality. These causal exchanges can be enacted while segregation in place and in spirit is maintained.

One way to demonstrate that *agape* and *eros* are compatible with segregation is to show how certain very segregationist frames of mind and practices are compatible with *agape* and *eros*. At the extreme the *agape* lover can appear to be saying: "You poor slob. You really need me, don't you? So I will give you a little of my superior value, and you should be grateful." This is demoralizing for the beloved—in this case, the black; it is no wonder that the black began to ask whether this love was designed for the seller's market only, and began to call in the 1960's for black pride. *Agape* can function as imperialism functions: It refers to its action in euphemistic language, speaking of wars of liberation, foreign aid, or manifest destiny; but it functions to structure the beloved "have nots" according to the specifications of the "haves." There is here an agapic dynamic, but clearly there is no social solidarity.

Eros can be a converse form of manipulation, whereby the lover seeks to acquire the values of the beloved. Sometimes the *eros* lover seeks to acquire the labor value of the beloved. Here *eros* can function as the exploitation of the worker is said to function in Marxism. The same erotic dynamic can be seen in the international exploitation by the "have" nations of the resources and labor of the "have not" nations.

Our point is not to pin the labels of imperialism and exploitation on *agape* and *eros*. Our point, rather, is to say that the dynamics of imperialism and exploitation are consistent extrapolations of *agape* and *eros*, and these dynamics should serve to demonstrate that *agape* and *eros* do not require integration, that in fact they are compatible with segregation. Imperialism is clearly an act between nations that are removed from each other. Imperialism between entities united in a social solidarity is inconceivable. The same can be said of exploitation. Imperialism and exploitation are actions that require the segregation of the lover and beloved, yet they exercise a form—admittedly, an extreme form—of the dynamics of *agape* and *eros.*

Of course, the actual dynamics of *agape* and *eros* are not usually so extreme, and they often exist amid social solidarity. For example, *agape* and *eros* are not only possible among the members of a family, they may be actually encouraged by the familial solidarity. Nevertheless, because *agape* and *eros* and imperialism and exploitation can coexist, it is obvious that *agape* and *eros* do not describe what is necessary to integration.

Our claim is that the ideal of aesthetic love does describe what is necessary to integration. We would make the additional claim that aesthetic love or any notion of love which can describe integration might itself foster the practice of that integration. Part of the racial predicament in the United States might be that whites are familiar only with notions of love which, at their extreme, suggest manipulative practices between isolated entities.

Before we move to the next illustration, two comments are in order. First, as we said earlier, we are not arguing that *agape* and *eros* have no legitimate roles in race relations. Obviously, a powerful group, such as the whites, must give some of what it controls to an oppressed group, such as the blacks. Similarly, a favored and isolated group, such as the whites, must become aware of the values of the blacks. Second, these comments have been spoken from the point of view of the white lover primarily because the speaker is white and is not prepared to speak from the point of view of the black lover.

3. *Education.* Jesus and Plato each had a pedagogy and each had a notion of love. And for both Jesus and Plato teaching was a species of the genus *love.* Their notions of love each described a form of human relationship, and their teaching was a particular expression of that particular form of human relationship.

But before we describe the *agape* pedagogy of Jesus and the *eros* pedagogy of Plato, we should note that both pedagogies are designed to serve a purpose. That purpose is to convey understanding so that, upon the completion of the educational event, someone who previously lacked understanding has acquired it.

Jesus teaches when he imparts the Word. Teaching is the giving of valuable news to those in need of that news. In the Synoptic Gospels Jesus comes saying essentially two things:[12] (1) The Kingdom of God is at hand, and (2) Prepare for the Kingdom by doing the will of God. Jesus spoke with authority; he brought the truth. Those who heard him were in need. If they did not receive and accept the word that he brought, they would be passed over when the Kingdom arrived. Jesus' work is an agapic gift of value from the lover to the beloved, who is in need. It is similarly obvious that this *agape* pedagogy is descriptive of an important contemporary practice of teaching, where the instructor is thought to be knowledgeable, the student is thought to be in need of knowledge, and education is thought of as the passing of knowledge from the former to the latter.

There is a purpose and a transfer of value in the pedagogy of Plato also. In this pedagogy the teacher is the erotic lover, the student is the beloved, and the transfer of value is from the beloved student to the loving teacher. It is the teacher who has need of understanding and it is the student who is endowed with understanding. In the *Theaetetus*, Plato has Socrates characterize himself as a midwife. A midwife helps those who are pregnant to give birth. Socrates, with a trace of irony, but with a fundamental seriousness, says, "I am so far like the midwife that I cannot myself give birth to wisdom, and the common reproach is true, that, though I question others, I can myself bring nothing to light because there is no wisdom in me."[13] The students, on the other hand, have "many admirable truths" "discovered by themselves from within." The delivery of the truths, however, is possible only through the assistance of Socrates. The role of the midwife corresponds to the role of the erotic lover, as that is described in the *Symposium*. In the *Symposium* the lover is one who lacks that which he or she loves, while the beloved has what the lover lacks, and love is the acquisition of the beloved's value by the lover.[14] The education of the lover progresses up a scale of perfection, up the heavenly ladder, from the love of lower to the love of higher objects of love, from bodies to forms of bodies to beauties of the soul to the love of laws, institutions, sciences, and philosophy, until finally the lover regards, as the beloved, "beauty's very self." In the *Phaedrus* erotic love is described by reference to the myth of the journey of the soul. The soul has known true being in the heavens. But a certain turmoil has caused her to fall from the heights of heaven to our world of more semblance. The soul forgets the truth witnessed earlier in the heavens. But when, in our world below, the soul perceives the physical beauty of some other being, the soul's memory of the true being in the heavens is slowly revived. The process of reviving memory is the basis of an educational theory: the teacher attempts to awaken a student's original wisdom and, in turn, to benefit by the student's eventual enunciation of that wisdom.[15]

The Socratic education is erotic. There is an analogy between this process and the method adopted in modern college seminars and discussion classes: the instructor, as the lover, asks questions, and the student, as the beloved, answers questions. Together they adopt an erotic relationship.

The pedagogies of Jesus and Plato are purposive in the sense that they seek to transfer knowledge so that in the future one who was ignorant will have gained understanding. And the full span of linear history is involved in this purposive transaction of understanding. The Word was "in the beginning," but was forgotten. Then it was imparted to the disciples, who, in turn, are instructed to go out and become *agape* teachers, making "disciples of all nations." Similarly, not only does the Socratic student receive wisdom from the earlier, heavenly beginnings; that student is to become a future and beloved source of wisdom for the state by becoming a politician.[16] So the purposive transactions of *agape* and *eros* education begin at the creative beginning of all and extend into the indefinite future.

In fact, the thoroughgoing purposiveness of both pedagogies qualifies them as instrumentalist or utilitarian forms of education. The education in neither instance is valuable in itself; it is valuable only as it somehow improves the future by giving understanding to one who was ignorant. And who is to deny the importance of utilitarian education?

But perhaps it is a mistake to believe that all education must always be justified in terms of some purpose aiming at the future. We have learned from the theory of entropy, that the physical universe will, in a finite quantity of time, become useless energy. All consequences will be, after all, inconsequential. Some people have come to believe that single lives do not persist, but perish. So always to work exclusively for a purpose may be, finally, to work for what is eventually nothing.

In other words, there is a need for a third pedagogy, a pedagogy of purposelessness. Such a pedagogy would look to the present intellectual commune among the students, teachers, and sources, and find that commune valuable in itself, rather than for the purpose it serves in the future. Such a pedagogy would be sufficiently self-confident to assert that education may be valuable in the way that football and the movies are valuable, that education need not necessarily be valuable exclusively in the way that calisthenics and brushing one's teeth are valuable. Teachers and students, when serving this ideal of education, would regard ideas not primarily in terms of their consequences, but as sounds in a concert created by students, teachers, and sources, a concert created by bringing into coherent dialogue the diverse insights of the various participants. This concert would be appreciated, as concerts ordinarily are, primarily for its present hearing.[17]

Ironically, this form of education, which ostensibly neglects the future, is often very productive for the future. There is ample evidence to indicate that thinkers whose work is exceptionally creative tend to view their work as play. They are primarily engrossed not by the prospect of results but by the aesthetic satisfaction acquired in the process of this inquiry.[18]

Our contention is that a purposeless education can be interpreted as a species of aesthetic love. Not only is it intrinsically valuable in the present moment, as aesthetic love is; it is, in addition, a social rather than an individualistic reality. Education determined by the structures of *agape* or *eros* has to do with passing value from the individual who has value to the individual who has need, and whose need will be met when the value is later received. A purposeless education has to do with a present, social conjunction of thought among students, teachers, and sources. The purposeless education would also, like aesthetic love, be evaluated aesthetically. This evaluation would refer to the satisfaction received by students and instructors from the conjunction of thought. That satisfaction would probably depend on the diversity of ideas held together in that social conjunction.

Finally, it is the purposelessness of this education which should be emphasized. It is an education which might be attentive to the fact that time is running out, and to the fact that we have been devoting our energies to overcoming the negativities. It is an education which might seek a respite, which might seek a positive experience. It is an education which would aspire to provide, before it is too late, intellectual satisfaction, presently felt.

Those, then, constitute our empirical illustrations. We have a few concluding words about subsequent lectures, but, prior to those, are there any questions from the audience? I await your questions.

Does no one have anything to say?

Surely someone has something to say.

A YOUNG SEMINARIAN *(from the back of the lecture hall):* Why are you calling these "empirical illustrations"?

SPEAKER: Do you question whether these are empirical illustrations?

YOUNG SEMINARIAN: Well, yes, I do. They seem a little imprecise.

SPEAKER: I had hoped that these illustrations would refer to immediate experience in the way fiction is said to refer to immediate experience. Fiction, after all, is a hypothetical construction of the actual world. And one sign of its success is the reader's willingness to say, "That's right. That's the way it is," and the reader's unwillingness to say, "Bull." If you can say, "That's right," then my illustrations are empirical. If you can say, "That's love," then I will have shown that certain types of love, and in particular, aesthetic love, are corroborated by common sense.

YOUNG SEMINARIAN: Don't you have a more technical defense than that?

SPEAKER: Would it be better if I were to refer to philosophy?

YOUNG SEMINARIAN: Maybe.

SPEAKER: It was Alfred North Whitehead who said that philosophy's "ultimate appeal is to the general consciousness of what in practice we experience."[19]

Our hope was that the listener might hear our illustrations and react with approval and grant that he or she has a general consciousness of a practice of aesthetic love. Our intention is not to try to invent a practice of love; it is merely to argue that a practice is in need of a name.

YOUNG SEMINARIAN: But this is just description. Your modesty is exposing you. You have posed as a theorist in theology, but you have worked yourself out of a job. You have left yourself nothing normative to tell the world.

SPEAKER: On the contrary, my good seminarian, you have just betrayed a distrust of the world, typical of those in your calling.

YOUNG SEMINARIAN: How is that?

SPEAKER: You have assumed that theology must be didactically normative to be theology, that it must instruct the world in what it never knew or has forgotten. To be didactically normative is to have no faith in the world. It is to presume that mere description tells of a world without norm or value. It is to presume that the world as it is, is void of God.

I would sooner take another gamble. I would like to think that one can be descriptive and normative about the world in the same breath, that there is something about the world that warrants affirmation, and that that is evident to observation. If the normative is in that sense evident, then it must be possible to note its presence by mere description. One who works out of such a premise will be sufficiently naïve to say: If I tell the truth, that will be normative.

YOUNG SEMINARIAN: For you, illustrations are a form of revelation, so, of course, they are imprecise! For you, common sense and human action are a source of religious truth, and that is simply natural theology!

SPEAKER: Is that bad? Natural theology does study the

ancient religion, but not as one studies an authority. For natural theology, present evidence is authoritative. Now look at conventional theology. It regards the ancient religion as the authority and it seeks to make that authority prevail in the present. But the present is a strange habitation for ancient truths. The present is so strewn with the ruins of our hopes and visions, our collapsed reasons, that the gleaming pillars of ancient faith seem incongruous.

YOUNG SEMINARIAN: Is conventional theology so bad?

SPEAKER: What's more, such theology, in its effort to cope with the present, tries to forget that the ancient past is not as solid as it is said to be. Such theology refuses to remember that in this universe, expanding at almost the speed of light; in this galaxy, which is one of a billion galaxies; near this sun, which is one of this galaxy's billion suns; on this planet, in a particular past era, in a particular culture, in a particular locale, a few aging males of average intelligence said that the meaning of the entire universe was this, and not that—and now this is remembered as the Word.

YOUNG SEMINARIAN: It is easy for you to caricature conventional theology's interest in the past. But does natural theology suffer any less from its commitment to the present?

SPEAKER: Natural theology not only is committed to the present; it resides in the present. It refuses to treat the ancient Word as an iron mandate, lashed to the present, whatever the present may be. But neither will natural theology disregard the ancient Word. It will treat the ancient Word as a suggestion, a hypothesis, which will be tested, even through illustrations, by an appeal to contemporary evidence.

YOUNG SEMINARIAN: But what is left of religion in such a scheme? Your natural theology will be a scholar's plaything. It cannot refer to a live religion.
SPEAKER: Religion is whatever it is that enables you to answer this question: Why get out of bed in the morning? And the natural theologian may be the one who gets out of bed in the morning in order to learn why one should get out of bed in the morning. And the natural theologian may hope to so use the ancient hypothesis to interpret the contemporary world that one day it will be possible to get out of bed and announce: I have dreamed and found reasons too.

We are saying here that one reason for getting out of bed in the morning is because love may be something more than a means for removing evil. It may also be something positive.
YOUNG SEMINARIAN: Do you claim you will be doing theology in the succeeding lectures too?
SPEAKER: Yes, in certain special and academic ways. I will tell you how, if you can bear a little more. Can you bear a little more?
YOUNG SEMINARIAN: Just barely.

There are particular reasons for calling what we do theology; in fact, there is a special reason pertinent to each ensuing lecture.

The second lecture, "Western Theology and Aesthetic Love," is theological for reasons of etiquette. The fact is that, in the Western world, it is in the discipline of conventional theology where the most sustained and intensive discussion of the nature of love has occurred. To fail to tip the hat to that heritage of thought would be, to say the least, rude. However, in this case more than etiquette is involved, for there seem to be real precedents in Western theology for what we are calling aesthetic love. Some of these precedents are merely apparent, but other precedents are actual; and the former must be distinguished from the latter. For purposes of brevity only, the lecture will discuss only a few theologians of the twentieth century.

The third lecture, "Ethics and Aesthetic Love," is theological for reasons of nostalgia. This lecture is theological because it seeks to demonstrate that aesthetic love in fact supports *agape*. This effort may grow out of a bad conscience. Or it may grow out of the inability to let go of an awkward question: With all this emphasis on the value for the self derived from aesthetic love, what happens to the traditional Christian ethical emphasis on the value the self gives to others? We will try to answer this question by showing how aesthetic love aids and abets *agape*.

The fourth lecture, "Solitude and Aesthetic Love," is theological for reasons of expediency. We have argued that *agape* and *eros* isolate the lover from the beloved because *agape* and *eros* are causal relations. And we have claimed that aesthetic love does not isolate lovers from each other—that, in fact, it makes possible a social reality—because aesthetic love is a noncausal relation. But we have not explained how a noncausal relation is possible. Such an explanation is needed because relations are normally interpreted causally. But if anything like a sufficient explanation is to be given, then something like a fundamental way of describing human contact, a way at variance from the causal way, must be set forth. Now very fundamental descriptions are metaphysical descriptions. So we anticipate the need for a metaphysical description. But to complicate the problem, we can see no way of providing a metaphysical description sufficient for explaining noncausal relations short of a metaphysical description that includes a notion of God. It would be awkward to call this effort at description philosophical, because contemporary philosophy simply does not have much of a place for metaphysics, and especially not for metaphysics with a God. But theology still has a place for both; hence, the expediency of calling this effort at explanation theological.

The fifth and last lecture, "Boredom and Aesthetic Love," is theological for reasons of necessity. There will be about this lecture nothing that smacks of etiquette, nostalgia or mere expediency, nothing very relaxed. By the time we reach the last lecture it will be apparent that one more step is mandatory. We will have acknowledged that there are theological precedents for what we have called aesthetic love, but that they have not described the phenomenon sufficiently. So the movement cannot stop with them. We will have noted that aesthetic love can serve *agape,* but this is primarily an aside to a venerable tradition. So the movement cannot stop there. We will have argued that only something like a theological metaphysic can cope with the predicament of isolation and alienation created by exclusively causal approaches to human relations. But, beyond this, one more step must be taken. For by that point we will not yet have addressed directly those who have long since acknowledged the fall, and the propriety of love after the fall, but who see little basis for affirmation. Such persons have no intimations of a positive love, a love before the fall, which might provide a positive reason for living. They are not so much pessimistic as they are bored—or without positive reasons. So, in order to show how aesthetic love might overcome this special boredom, we must show how aesthetic love has sufficient value to deal with boredom. But how this necessity for an answer is finally a necessity for a theological answer—that question must wait until the last lecture, which will discuss the aesthetic value of religion.

SPEAKER TO THE SAME YOUNG SEMINARIAN: Shall we shake hands on the venture?
YOUNG SEMINARIAN: You mean I should come forward?
SPEAKER: Would not a handshake be an act of human contact?
YOUNG SEMINARIAN: Well, of course.
SPEAKER: Could we not call it an act of love?
YOUNG SEMINARIAN: If you want to.
SPEAKER: Would it be a Christian or a Greek handshake?
YOUNG SEMINARIAN: Are you serious?
SPEAKER: Always. Would I give my valuable hand to you in the spirit of Christian *agape,* to meet your aching need for a handshake? Would my shake of your hand be beneficent, compassionate, or sacrificial?
YOUNG SEMINARIAN: I hope not.
SPEAKER: Would I take your hand in an act of desire, a desire driven by my need for your blushing, tender palm? Would my handshake be Greek and erotic?
YOUNG SEMINARIAN: That's awful.
SPEAKER: Would my hand actively shake your passive hand? Or would your hand be the activist, shaking my passive hand?

YOUNG SEMINARIAN: Neither, obviously.

SPEAKER: Would the handshake be causal, in the sense that one hand would be the cause of the shaking action and the other hand's shaking would be the effect? Or would this shake be temporal, in that one hand would act in one moment of time and the other would react in a later moment?

YOUNG SEMINARIAN: Don't be silly.

SPEAKER: Would the handshake be American at all?

YOUNG SEMINARIAN: How do you mean, American?

SPEAKER: Would it be pragmatic, utilitarian, or instrumental? Would it seek to function as a present means for the accomplishment of something in the future?

YOUNG SEMINARIAN: I thought handshakes were merely friendly. If I thought there were an angle, I would keep my hand by my side.

SPEAKER: Do you know what's interesting about acts of touching?

YOUNG SEMINARIAN: No. But can I send out for hot dogs?

SPEAKER: No hot dogs. I am almost through. With tactile contact, you see, there is no space between the places which touch. Without space, there is no motion, because motion occurs through space. Without motion there is no time, because time is a measurement of an interval of motion.[20] Now handshakes require the contact of palms; they avoid spatial separation, motion, and time. A handshake would make our hands contemporaries, "in touch" in the same moment of time. So the hands would be together, in social commune, as it were.

Now, we could talk about the aesthetic qualities of various handshakes.

YOUNG SEMINARIAN: Enough!

II:
Western Theology and Aesthetic Love

Ladies and Gentlemen:

Speculation on love is a little like an archaeological dig. To speculate on love is not to invent love, any more than an archaeologist can invent a lost city. Both activities discover something already there. What is more, both the speculator and the archaeologist must first determine where to search for a discovery, and then, after the discovery is made, describe it properly.

We have already begun the task of describing aesthetic love, and we have said how that description is to be evaluated. The description of love is to be evaluated by the only informed authorities there are: the lovers, using their common sense. The archaeologist's conclusions are assessed by the only informed authorities there are: the historians, using their expertise. But lover and historian are uniquely qualified to evaluate, because they are evaluating something that has to do with themselves. In their assessment of theories of human love, the lovers must continually consult what love is and can be for themselves. The historians must remember that the lost city was inhabited by humans too, and that it can be understood only when the historians, as humans, identify with their subjects. Each evaluator must ask, How can this discovery make sense to a human like myself, who has certain needs and an orderly mind? Can I think the thoughts implied by this discovery?

However, prior to the description and the evaluation, the speculator and the archaeologist must first determine where to search for the discovery. Guidance in finding the discovery must always come from those who have wondered and dug before. This lecture is an acknowledgment of that guidance in the discovery of aesthetic love.

So we will move beyond description and the corroboration from common sense and look to the theological community, which has been speculating about love for millennia. The work of this community has set precedents for thought about love, and much can be learned from a look at those precedents. From that community we can find where to begin the theological dig.

Our first task is to determine the method for finding the theological dig for aesthetic love. There is a clue in our earlier description of aesthetic love. If aesthetic love has been described as noncausal, nontemporal and nonindividual, then it is most likely that such love can be found in the locations where noncausality, nontemporality, and nonindividuality prevail. Our task may not be difficult. There cannot be very many precedents for aesthetic love, because the area where noncausality, nontemporality and nonindividuality prevail is, in the Western world, quite restricted. The larger domain is ruled by causality, temporality, and individuality.[1]

Even with this method, however, mistakes can be made. There are apparent precedents for aesthetic love, and they seem natural to the special area where aesthetic love should be found. However, on closer inspection they turn out not to be precedents for aesthetic love, but artifacts from another theological dig.

Nevertheless, this method can locate the actual precedents that seem natural to the special area, and that, in fact, are.

The apparent precedents will be represented primarily by a book by Daniel Day Williams, and the actual precedents will be represented by writings of Martin Buber, Paul Tillich, and a nontheologian, Erich Fromm.

The Apparent Precedents

Mutual love seems to be a precedent for aesthetic love because it seems to presuppose the notion of nonindividuality, or sociality. How mutual love presupposes nonindividuality can be explained, however, only after a preliminary definition of mutual love. This definition will refer to the most famous recent advocate of mutual love, Reinhold Niebuhr.

According to Niebuhr, mutual love is based on reciprocation; it is a "tit for tat" love. It says, I will do this for you, if you do that for me. But, finally, it is pushed to say, If I know you will not reciprocate, then I will not do this for you.

Niebuhr selectively advocated mutual love as an alternative to *agape*. He looked at the fate of Jesus and concluded that if you practice *agape* in the social arena, you could well get killed. Niebuhr believed that, in principle, *agape* is ethically superior to mutual love, but that in practice, when dealing with the large political and economic events in our current history, *agape's* selfless giving may be suicidal or at least self-defeating. Sometimes such an act may be a moral mistake because it means that the ethically superior forces may be destroyed. Since the practice of mutual love insists on the protection of self-interest, in some sort of balance of power, the lover is less likely to be defeated or destroyed. The insistence on reciprocation makes mutual love sometimes morally warranted.[2]

Now this insistence on reciprocation seems to presuppose the predominance of nonindividuality, or of social relatedness. And that would seem to ally mutual love with aesthetic love.

Certainly, the insistence on reciprocation distinguishes mutual love from *agape* and *eros.* Both *agape* and *eros* can be enacted by the lover alone, and be met with no active response. One can give and be met with ingratitude and one still actualizes *agape;* in fact one is told to give with no thought of return, one is told to expect the gift to be sheerly sacrificial. Or one can desire, or seek to take, and be met with indifference, and one still actualizes *eros;* in fact, in matters of romance, unrequited *eros* is the archetypal affair. The classic expressions of *agape* and *eros* make it apparent that not only are *agape* and *eros* possible without reciprocation; without reciprocation they are improved, intensified, raised to their highest pitch. Mutual love, on the other hand, is not undertaken without a prior prediction about the beloved's response; and that prediction must be that the beloved will reciprocate positively —or the mutual love will not begin.

Now it is this attentiveness to social circumstances which prompts the question, Is mutual love a precedent for aesthetic love? After all, aesthetic love also rejects individualism, the individualism which says that the lover's action alone is determinative of the love. Aesthetic love, if it is to exist at all, requires the participation of others beside the lover. Mutual love cannot tolerate a one-sided, or immutual, interpretation of human relations any more than aesthetic love can. In the illustrations in the first lecture, mutual love would usually have sided with aesthetic love. For example, there we noted that aesthetic love would differ from an agapic interpretation of sex, which describes sex in terms of the lover's sacrificial giving, and from an erotic interpretation of sex, which describes sex in terms of the lover's desirous taking. Mutual love would similarly reject these interpretations and insist on a mutuality of act and response, of response and act, in sex. Neither would mutual love, any more than aesthetic love, tolerate the one-sided manipulation of the weak by the powerful, whether that be the quasi-imperialistic giving of value or the quasi-exploitative taking of value. Again, mutual love would call for a mutuality of the dynamics of giving and taking.

The question remains then: Does mutual love's insistence on reciprocation represent a dependence on the notion of nonindividuality? And does that make mutual love a precedent for aesthetic love?

This question can be answered only by a closer look at mutual love. Such a look reveals that mutual love is informed by causality, temporality and, not nonindividuality, but individuality. Consequently, mutual love cannot be a precedent for aesthetic love.

Daniel Day Williams' version of mutual love, which he calls "communion," makes this clear. It pictures communion in terms of two movements, an active and a passive (a "suffering") movement. Williams describes the active movement as "self-giving" because it is the active giving by the self for the benefit of the other. He describes the passive movement as self-affirming because it is the receiving from the other of something beneficial to the self:

> Both self-affirmation and self-giving are aspects of the essential love which is the will to communion. Self-affirmation without response is deadly. That is why egoism so often becomes desperate. Self-giving without self-affirmation is meaningless. That is why much of what appears to be self-giving love is really self-destruction. What we need to see is that self-affirmation and self-giving are united in the essence of love which is communion.[3]

These two movements are necessary to any version of mutual love, because mutual love's reciprocation means that each party to the love must give value to the other and receive value from the other.

Williams' communion, like all versions of mutual love, involves an exchange of value, and, as such, it involves causality, temporality, and individuality. Always in mutual love one person must causally impart a gift and the other must receive the causal effect of that gift.[4] Equally, temporality is always involved: one person initiates the act in one moment of time and the other receives it at a later moment of time. And, despite what we have said about the nonindividuality of mutual love, it is individualistic. Because the mutual lover works causally and temporally, he or she stands alone, isolated from the beloved, in an earlier or later moment of time. This is true despite the fact that the mutual lover is responsive, in each succeeding moment, to what the beloved has done in the preceding moment.

It is apparent that Williams' active movement of love is analogous to *agape;* an active self-giving is exactly what *agape* is. The passive movement is correlative to *eros;* while the act of *eros* is an active solicitation and not passive, *eros* does aim to reach that point where it can passively receive the beloved's value.

This surprising interpretation of the structure of mutual love is corroborated by a look at the history of mutual love in Christian thought. Williams places his own thinking about communion within a heritage of thought about love that begins with Augustine.[5] And this Augustinian heritage is, in the last analysis, a tradition wherein *agape* and *eros* are combined.[6] Augustine himself combined them in the following way: Humans should seek God in all things, with *eros.* But humans are erotically attracted to the sensual things themselves, rather than to the presence of God in them. So, to foster the proper *eros,* God's presence was self-given in the incarnation. This was an act of *agape* that fostered human *eros* for God. Martin D'Arcy is the major modern exponent of the Augustinian combination of *agape* and *eros.* In *The Mind and the Heart of Love,* D'Arcy says:

> There is a desire of the self to give its all and a desire to be oneself and be perfect. The principle of give and take has to be harmonized in all phases of love.[7]

D'Arcy correlates the giving movement with altruism, centrifugal love, the feminine, *anima,* and *agape;* he correlates the taking movement with egocentricity, centripetal love, the masculine, *animus,* and *eros.*[8]

Mutual love then is a two-headed creature. It can act in two different ways, and that is more than *agape* or *eros* can do. But, finally, mutual love must move as one body. At any moment, in any particular situation, it must function either as *agape* or as *eros*. Consequently, in any particular act it differs from aesthetic love just as *agape* and *eros* do. Mutual love, in short, may appear to be a precedent for aesthetic love, but it is not.[9]

The Actual Precedents

What we seek are the actual precedents, those notions of love which appear to be precedents for aesthetic love and, in fact, are.

We have sought the precedents by attempting to look in the special area where the characteristics of noncausality, nontemporality, and nonindividuality prevail. We attempted to find a notion of love natural to that area by finding a notion of love with one or more of those three characteristics implicit in it, the hope being that we could proceed to demonstrate that the entire notion of love belonged to that special area. This technique is loose; in fact, it has just failed us.

We need a technique for better indicating which notions of love really belong in the restricted area. Rather than hunt for a notion of love with one or more of the three characteristics, we will hunt for an intermediate tradition, a set of notions less fundamental than the metaphysical ideas of noncausality, nontemporality, and nonindividuality, but more fundamental than any particular notion of love. In addition, this tradition should presuppose the three metaphysical ideas. If we can first identify such a tradition, and then find certain theories of love that depend on it, we may have located certain actual precedents for aesthetic love.

Western mysticism is just such an intermediate phenomenon; as a tradition it does presuppose noncausality, nontemporality, and nonindividuality. In fact, mysticism may be an unconventional phenomenon in the West because it depends on those uncommon metaphysical ideas. Mysticism is also one foundation for three recent Western theories of love.

We will begin by showing how Western mysticism presupposes noncausality, nontemporality, and nonindividuality. D. T. Suzuki, writing about Meister Eckhart's mysticism, says:

> God is not in time mathematically enumerable. His creativity is not historical, not accidental, not at all measurable. It goes on continuously without cessation with no beginning, with no end. It is not an event of yesterday or today or tomorrow, it comes out of timelessness, of nothingness, of Absolute Void. God's work is always done in an absolute present, in a timeless "now which is time and place in itself." God's work is sheer love, utterly free from all forms of chronology and teleology. The idea of God creating the world out of nothing, in an absolute present, and therefore altogether beyond the control of a serial time conception will not sound strange to Buddhist ears.[10]

This rejection of conventional temporality is so fundamental to mysticism that it makes causality, in any conventional Western sense, impossible. It obviates, as Suzuki says, chronology and teleology, and without those notions causality is senseless. Equally, mysticism rejects individuality. Oriental mysticism affirms such a complete unity of the self with the divine that the self is negated. Western mysticism rejects individualism in a less extreme way: The self stands not in union with the divine, but in communion with the divine; the self does participate in the divine presence, but the identity of the self is retained.[11] However, even in Western mysticism strict individuality is overcome by commune; fullest self-realization is attained, not in solitariness, but in a relatedness with the divine.

Several recent theories of love depend on this minor tradition of Western mysticism. Martin Buber, Paul Tillich, and Erich Fromm each enunciated theories of love that were influenced by mysticism. As a consequence of this influence, none of their theories of love depend heavily on causality, temporality, or individuality.

For Martin Buber, love is something within the I-You relationship. According to Buber, there are two basic forms of relationship: the I-It relationship and—depending on which translation is cited—the I-Thou or the I-You relationship. In the I-You relationship the total self confronts the other in its totality. In the I-It relationship the self experiences the other; that is, the self attends with part of itself (its feeling, perception, imagination, wants, senses, thoughts) to some particular aspect of the other.[12] In the I-It relationship what is called love is only some expression or feeling had by and within the self and directed toward the other. But real love is found in the I-You relationship, and that love suffuses the self and the other or it exists between the self and the other.

> Feelings dwell in man, but man dwells in his love.
> This is no metaphor but actuality: love does not

cling to an I, as if the You were merely its "content" or object; it is between I and You.[13]

Buber says that the love which exists between the I and the You is a "cosmic force." And it is here that the mystical foundation of Buber's notion of love is apparent. Buber, referring to this cosmic force, this God, as the eternal You, says:

> Extended, the lines of relationship intersect in the eternal You.
>
> Every single You is a glimpse of that. Through every single You the basic word addresses the eternal You. The mediatorship of the You of all beings accounts for the fullness of our relationships to them.[14]

The eternal You is the link between the I and the You. The peculiarities of this mystical link are what makes the love between the I and the You noncausal, nontemporal, and peculiarly nonindividual.

Buber's God functions noncausally, while the Gods of *agape* and *eros* function causally, either as efficient or as final cause. The eternal You is like "the air in which you breathe."[15] It is the indispensable medium between the I and the You, but it does not causally initiate that love. The Gods of *agape* and *eros* do causally initiate those loves. The God of *agape* is like a push pump, and the God of *eros* is like a suction pump. Anders Nygren, commenting on God's function in *agape*, and paraphrasing Martin Luther, says:

> He [the Christian] has nothing of his own to give. He is merely the tube, the channel, through which God's love flows.[16]

And it is God which impels the flow of love through the tube. Nygren goes on to quote Augustine, who also uses a metaphor about fluids, but to describe the flow of *eros:*

> Conduct the water which is flowing into the sewer, to the garden instead. Such a strong urge as it had to the world, let it have to the Creator of the world.[17]

It is the Creator who instills in humans that erotic urge toward the Creator; so God, in effect, draws the flow of erotic love. Augustine, says Nygren, describes an upward flow, from the *eros* lover, through the beloved, to the enjoyment of God, whereas Luther describes a downward flow from God, through the *agape* lover to the beloved. In either case, however, God functions to initiate a causal movement.

The nature of God's function in making a particular kind of love possible can determine the nature of that love. The Gods of *agape* and *eros* function causally and imprint those loves with a causal character. The God of Buber's I-You relationship functions as a mystical, or spiritual, medium between the I and the You. There is no causality in that and, consequently, no causal character to the love between the I and the You. So *agape* and *eros* function by the causalities of giving and taking, but the I-You love involves no such causal transaction, nor, as a consequence, does it involve temporality or individual isolation.[18]

Buber explicitly denies the role of causality in the I-You relationship:

> Here I and You confront each other freely in a reciprocity that is not involved in or tainted by any causality.[19]

No purpose intervenes between I and You, no greed and no anticipation. . . . Every means is an obstacle. Only where all means have disintegrated encounters occur.[20]

Buber is equally explicit in denying that the I-You relationship deals with past or future individuals[21] and in claiming that "Only as the You becomes present does presence come into being."[22]

Similarly, the love in the I-You relationship overcomes an isolated individuality. Buber refers to the world of I-You relationships as the "world of relation," and distinguishes that from the "world of experience," where one steps out of relations and makes the other into a remote object.[23] In the I-You relationship the I and the You stand in relation, "in the sacred basic word."[24]

Our contention is that the spiritual medium—which is the love that lies between the I and the You—has made possible these characteristics of noncausality, nontemporality, and nonindividuality. Because Buber's I-You relationship has these three characteristics, it is an actual precedent for aesthetic love.

The mystical base of Buber's notion of love is Hasidism, a popular Jewish communal mysticism, begun in the eighteenth century in eastern Europe. Buber says Hasidism is "a realistic and active mysticism, i.e., a mysticism for which the world is not an illusion, from which man must turn away in order to reach true being."[25] Hasidism is a mysticism that recognizes the Eternal implicit in the temporal, especially in the self's "holy intercourse with all existing beings."[26]

While Paul Tillich was not explicitly associated with

a mystical movement, it is apparent that he stands in a line of Western mystics or quasi mystics such as Plotinus, Pseudo-Dionysius, and Jakob Böhme.[27] The mystical aspect of Tillich's own thought is most evident in his notion of God as the "Spiritual Presence."[28] With Tillich also it is the mystical element which makes the theory of love noncausal, nontemporal, and nonindividual.

God, according to Tillich, can be thought of in terms of power, empowering all life, and in terms of form, in-forming all life; but these are merely abstractions about God, and they treat God statically. In actuality, God is living, in motion; and humans and all other beings relate to this living God, and not to the abstractions about God. If the power of God is correlative to God the Father and the form (or, *logos*) of God is correlative to God the Son, these are as abstractions compared to the actuality of God as life. The living God is present to humans as the Spiritual Presence; the Spiritual Presence is an alternative name for the Holy Spirit.[29]

It is the Spiritual Presence which "grasps" the human spirit and "takes" the human self into the life of God. When this occurs, the human self is ecstatically empowered and in-formed, so that it is enabled to do what otherwise it cannot do.[30]

> The spirit, a dimension of finite life, is driven into a successful self-transcendence; it is grasped by something ultimate and unconditional. It is still the human spirit; it remains what it is, but at the same time, it goes out of itself under the impact of the divine Spirit. "Ecstasy" is the classical term for this state of being grasped by the Spiritual Presence.[31]

The acceptance of this grasping and this ecstasy is faith. This acceptance of being "grasped" allows one to be "taken into" the life of God. To be taken into the life of God is to participate in a reuniting love. So Tillich says, "The consciousness of ultimate identity in the One makes identification with all beings possible and necessary."[32] This determination of faith and love by the Spiritual Presence of God makes faith and love basically mystical experiences.

The mystical influence on love can be understood pictorially. While Buber describes something analogous to a spiritual cloud around and between people, a cloud through which their contact is enabled, Tillich describes love as one phase in a movement analogous to the opening and closing movements of the points of calipers. Persons are individuals, the way points of calipers are individuals, even when they are touching; yet persons are not totally separated from, or strange to, each other—they are connected just as the points of calipers are connected through the moving arms and the hinge. The movement of the arms and hinge is analogous to the movement of the life of God. If these calipers are pictured as opening and closing, moments of love are any moments during the closing movement, the movement from separation to contact. Tillich calls love "reunion"; it is the communion of the separated.[33]

Persons are separated from each other for two reasons. First, they are properly separated; in essence, or ideally, persons are individuals and should periodically retreat to their separation from each other. But persons are also in essence, or ideally, in relation to each other. Here, on this ideal plane, love is the natural and proper reunion of persons naturally and properly separated.

But persons are also separated from each other because of sin; in existence, or actually, they are estranged from each other by a warped egocentricity. Love is, then, also the reunion of persons estranged from each other by a sinful separation.

But in either case—whether it overcomes either a natural and essential separation or an unnatural and sinful separation—reunion is a participation in the divine reuniting movement, which is absolutely fundamental to love itself. Love, in other words, is always participation in the life of God. It occurs only when human spirits are grasped and taken into the Spiritual Presence of the life of God. That ecstatic, or mystical, event is the foundation of human love. The love of people for each other is a movement toward each other, empowered and informed by the moving power and form of God, but the actual reception of the power and form is made possible by their mystical contact with God. It is persons' mystical commune with God which brings them together.

Finally, it is this mystical contact which makes Tillich's love noncausal, nontemporal, and nonindividual. Without this mystical participation in the life of God, persons would have to interact causally; but with that participation in the life of God persons can be noncausally related. Without this mystical participation, persons would have to interact through time sequentially and interact as individuals separated in earlier and later moments; but with that participation persons can interact communally in the present moment because they are simultaneously participating in the life of God.

So Tillich and Buber have notions of love that are actual precedents for aesthetic love.[34] And we have discovered that they can function as precedents because they each have a foundation in mysticism. Tillich can say, "Love is the state of being taken by the Spiritual Presence into the transcendent unity of unambiguous life."[35] And here he is reminiscent of Martin Buber, who can say, "The mediatorship of the You of all beings accounts for the fullness of our relationships to them."[36]

That concludes today's lecture. Are there any questions?

THE SAME YOUNG SEMINARIAN: Why did you omit Erich Fromm?

SPEAKER: You mean the famed psychologist?

YOUNG SEMINARIAN: Yes. You did promise that the actual precedents would be represented by Martin Buber, Paul Tillich, and Erich Fromm. But you have left out Erich Fromm.

SPEAKER: Did you take that as a promise?

YOUNG SEMINARIAN: I certainly did. At least what you said functioned for me as a promise might function.

SPEAKER: And how, in this case, did a promise function?

YOUNG SEMINARIAN: It caused me to keep my seat.

SPEAKER: But, you see, I knew you might not stay seated for mere theology. So what was I to do but promise you a word from a psychologist?

YOUNG SEMINARIAN: But why Fromm?

SPEAKER: To make it believable. Fromm did write a book on love entitled, *The Art of Loving*. And in that book he contended that the basic problem for humankind was not how to causally resolve needs, but how to deal with separateness.[37] He said that love meets this problem by providing "at-onement," or "interpersonal union."[38] And while Fromm is no theist, he referred with approval to mystical notions of God as the oneness[39] which unites humanity, and he said that the active appreciation of the oneness of humanity is the deepest expression of love.

YOUNG SEMINARIAN: You tricked me.

SPEAKER: Chastise me as you will. But what else was I to do? I wanted you to hear about the precedents.

III:
Ethics and Aesthetic Love

Ladies and Gentlemen:

There are those who would say that we have exaggerated the importance of aesthetic love, and they would be right.

They would remind us that most of the time love must work causally, through time, to aid those who stand in our literal future. They might refer to the planning and the utilitarian action designed to meet the needs of others, the needs to overcome war and strife, starvation and malnutrition, overpopulation and pollution, injustice and corruption. They might remind us that during the minutes and hours we have blathered on about aesthetic love with our affluent peers, during those very minutes and hours "three out of every four people in the developing world do not have enough calories."[1] And if they were to argue that these concerns make the exercise of *agape* urgent, they would be right.

They would add that we have neglected the virtues of humility and appreciation. They might say that we have overlooked our own ignorance and spiritual torpor just as we have underrated the insight and inspiration which others might give us. They might reason that aesthetic love among citizens of the materialistic West might be of limited value so long as the West remains innocent of the spiritual and aesthetic experience of the East. If they argued that *eros* should not be neglected, they would be right.

Agape and *eros*, they might say, encourage a concern for the needs and values of others, even others strange to us. But aesthetic love, taken by itself, might encourage an elitist mentality. It might so emphasize good times with one's peers that it would encourage the exclusion of strangers. Aesthetic love, they might say, is the first step on the way to the exclusiveness of the rich and the privileged and the powerful. Why, they might ask, could not aesthetic love function to justify the country club, the class system, or the clan?

They might contend that we have taken *agape* and *eros*, declared them the two great oxen of the Western world, set them up to be gored, and then made their supine carcasses a platform for our defense of aesthetic love. Can it be denied that there is some accuracy in this charge?

They would remind us that, whatever we have said earlier, *agape* and *eros* live. *Agape* and *eros* strive to build the future, whether that be the future reception of the *agape* lover's gift or the future resolution of the *eros* lover's desire. *Agape* and *eros* do, with pain and a faltering step, slowly pull our cart through time. The causal future is attained; and the anticipation and actions of *agape* and *eros* do contribute to its attainment.

We could raise the demurrer that neither must life aboard the oxcart, life in our creaky present, be forgotten. Else why stay aboard? Why be so glad that we have been pulled into the future, if that future, when it becomes a present reality, is always—always—ignored for the sake of some new concern for some future prospect. If there is never a regard for the quality of life in present actuality, then actual life will be ignored. *Agape* and *eros* make sense as instrumental values only if they aim toward somebody's eventual satisfaction in actual life. And aesthetic love is one instance of that satisfaction, for aesthetic love is love aboard the oxcart, among those in the present.

But, rather than pursue at this time the defense of aesthetic love, we will attend to the criticism. Is aesthetic love necessarily irresponsible to the future and to those who lie beyond our parochial circles? Certainly, aesthetic love is an end in itself, useful simply for being experienced. But can it also function instrumentally, as a means to some future good? Can it function ethically?

Our answer to this question will concentrate on how aesthetic love serves *agape*, rather than how it serves *eros*. The ethical responsibility to serve the needs of others seems more weighty than the ethical responsibility to erotically satisfy our own needs. Admittedly, the weight may fall there only for subjective reasons: it may be because our culture has officially emphasized the ethical importance of *agape* or because we feel guilty from our continuous neglect of those who suffer.

This lecture cannot be delivered at the construction site of aesthetic love. It must be delivered a few hundred feet away, where the sidewalk critics stand. They have asked us: "Is this really the time to try to put up a notion of aesthetic love? The planet is in crisis. We are witnessing the first stages of what is sure to be mass famine. Nuclear arms are held by more and more nations, and the temptation to use them increases each day as usable resources are depleted, as population growth soars out of control, and as the poor nations fall farther and farther behind the rich nations—just when the poor nations' expectations are rising. All this (the sidewalk critics might say)—all this and you are calling for aesthetic love, a love whose use is to bring satisfaction in the present moment of social interaction. Is this not rather the time to work causally to alleviate future suffering? Is this not the time for the favored few to work agapically to meet the needs of the deprived many? Is this not the worst time to look at the quality of the present moment? Now is the hour (the sidewalk critics might conclude) to abandon this new construction, to return to the site of *agape,* to encamp there, and to follow its blueprint for a more livable future!"

Responding to the sidewalk critics is difficult, because we are conscious of the soundness of their point. But we will attempt a response. Stated generally, it assumes the form of paradoxes: That love which seeks only intrinsic value has, nevertheless, instrumental value. That love which has no purpose, or has no intentions for the future, serves a purpose, anyway. That love which begins by separating itself from *agape* ends by serving *agape.*

Stated specifically, this response has two parts: first, aesthetic love enhances our *perception* of moral situations, because it accustoms us to view others as those with whom we are bonded, rather than as those who stand apart from us with needs; second, aesthetic love enhances our *motivation* to act morally, because it provides aesthetic satisfaction for responsible moral action. This is not to say that aesthetic love alters *agape* itself; rather, it is to say that aesthetic love may contribute to the personal resources of the one who attempts to exercise *agape.*

Moral Perception

The problem of perception may be best seen by reference to a particular phenomenon that Reinhold Niebuhr discusses in his *Moral Man and Immoral Society.* There he says that people tend to exercise *agape* with family and friends, but they abandon that selfless, giving love when they are dealing with large groups, such as nations.

Why do people abandon *agape* when they are dealing with large, impersonal groups? Is their failure to exercise *agape* only a moral failure, prompted entirely by a selfish disposition? Or might the failure be in part an accidental failure, prompted by a limited perception of the situation?

The validity of the latter explanation can be illustrated by a look at conflicting attitudes held by inhabitants of the United States toward two essentially similar situations. On one hand apartheid in the Republic of South Africa is deplored. The white South African's systematic oppression of the black, together with the nearly total segregation of the black from the white, is said to be morally outrageous. Yet the same people who condemn apartheid generally fail to see that we, as a rich nation, treat the poor nations much as the white South African treats the black South African. For just as the white South African denies the black South African the right to live in white areas, we deny inhabitants of poor nations access to our rich land through economic barriers and immigration quotas. Just as the white South African has denied the black South African the vote, we have denied poor nations a meaningful franchise by keeping the United Nations weak. Just as white South Africans maintain a seven-to-one wage gap between themselves and black South Africans, we maintain between ourselves and the poor nations a wage gap that is, on the whole, much larger. We accomplish this through tariffs and import quotas, through the cheap purchase of natural resources from poor nations, through minimal wages paid by U.S. industries located in poor nations, and, most of all, through refusing to share our wealth through foreign aid. Every year the U.S. federal budget is set, and every year it says essentially one thing: Yes to domestic affluence and military might, and No to assistance to the poor nations. But still—and this is the problem—the inhabitants of the United States do not perceive that what they are doing to the poor nations is morally outrageous.

Clearly, a higher moral demand is applied to the white South Africans, in their dealings with their compatriots, than is applied to the United States in its dealings with the poor nations. An agapic concern for the outcast is demanded of the white South African, but national selfishness is tolerated for the United States in its dealings with the poor nations. The toleration of U.S. selfishness cannot be explained exclusively in moral terms. Nationalistic pride is not the only cause of the citizens' inability to discern the nation's immorality. Rather, the toleration of U.S. selfishness is explained in part by an accidental limitation in the perception of the situation by the inhabitants of the United States.

That the problem is in part a problem of perception can be supported by a look at a crucial difference between the two situations. The inhabitants of the United States see the Republic of South Africa as a single national community. They see the blacks and the whites as belonging to the same national family, as being together in the same communal nexus. On the other hand, they do not naturally and immediately perceive that rich nations and poor nations belong to the same international family, that they all belong irrevocably in the same communal nexus.

Our contention is that there is an honest failure of perception; people really do not see the systemic and human unity of the global community, so the idea of global responsibility is not taken seriously. Certainly the failure is in part moral; to some extent the failure to perceive the communal reality is unnecessary and attributable to a sinful disposition. It is presently possible to perceive better than we do as a nation. Planned Parenthood–World Population does, and so does the American Friends Service Committee. But there is, in addition to the moral failure, an accidental failure of perception. A global, or international, community is more subtle, more difficult to see than a national community. And this difficulty is accidental because it is due largely to the fact that the international community is so large, geographically. This accidental difficulty causes problems in perception that, in turn, diminish moral judgment.

Look at the phenomenon of foreign aid. Aid by the rich nations to the poor nations is singularly appropriate. Where better could *agape* be practiced? Where is there a more pressing instance of those with value who could give to those with need? Admittedly, population growth rates complicate the problem and may indicate that food banks and other forms of international sharing will only delay the time when famine will come. In fact, certain forms of sharing may mean that when famine does come there will be more people to suffer.[2] However, aid that contributes to population stabilization and internal development is still quite feasible. Yet foreign aid is barely practiced: the United States gives through its federal government about one one thousandth of its gross national product in foreign aid. And where there are foreign aid programs, it is reported that they are usually riddled with corruption and incompetence.[3] U.S. foreign aid programs are too frequently designed to serve the military and economic self-interest of the United States, and the aid itself is often handed over with insulting and uninformed stipulations as to how it should be used.

The United States glorifies its generosity, and by that generosity it means the kind of giving which *agape* would call for. But the United States treats poor nations the way one would never dream of treating a friend. This failure must be due, at least in part, to a failure of perception. If it were due to moral perversity alone, why would that general perversity be directed so particularly to large, impersonal groups?

How can this failure of perception be corrected? It is doubtful if it will help greatly to tell people to look harder through the old spectacles of *agape*. It may help to give people a second pair of spectacles, however. If people were used to looking at the world with the norm of aesthetic love, they might become more capable of perceiving the communal reality of all situations, to see how even nations are bound to each other, within an international community. Then people might come to better perceive their agapic responsibility for those with whom they are communally bound.

The model of human relations implicit in the notion of *agape* might, in some cases, even diminish the very perception *agape* needs. *Agape* pictures humans as causally separated from one another: there is one who has value and gives value and there is another who has needs and must receive value, and that lover and that beloved are separated by their diverse circumstances and roles. With time this can lead to an illusion: the *agape* lover is a benefactor, one to whom gratitude and honor are due; the *agape* lover's gift bequeaths a privilege to the underprivileged; the *agape* lover is a privileged person, remote from the unwashed.

But if people's perceptions were also nourished by aesthetic love's estimate of the noncausal togetherness of people, this "distancing" of lover from beloved might be less likely. The *agape* lover might then more readily discern his or her responsibility, even for the beloved who is not a relative or a friend.

Moral Motivation

We said that aesthetic love could help the *agape* lover in a second way—by augmenting his or her motivation to perform *agape* love.

The Biblical story of the rich young ruler might be read as primarily a story about how unappealing *agape* is. Jesus asks the man to sell all he has and to give the money to the poor. This is a request that *agape* be performed, and the request is refused. That refusal has important implications. It means not only that the rich young ruler will never enter the Kingdom of God; it means also, and perhaps much more importantly, that the poor people, who should have received his wealth, will remain poor. But because *agape* is unappealing, people continue to reject the invitation to perform *agape* and they and those they might help continue to suffer the consequences. *Agape* does present a dour picture of the experience of loving. So some people, thinking that love means only sacrificing something present for the benefit of someone else in the future, do go on, like the rich young ruler, looking sad, turning their backs, kicking the dust and walking away. And the poor go on being poor.

The motivation to love, experienced by the *agape* lover, is not naturally strong. *Agape* has been described as a sacrificial love, and people who are not masochistic are not naturally motivated to be sacrificial. In the past they may have justified their present sacrifice with the hope that it was merely a temporary payment for a future and eternal bliss. But what happens when that hope is nullified because people lose a belief in anything like heaven? What happens when paradise is taken away? Should people be advised to continue sacrificing for the benefit of others, so that those others can be enabled to sacrifice in turn? And should this go on and on, unrelentingly, and should that be a model of meaningful human relations? Should we be surprised that the motivation to perform *agape* is weak? Should we be surprised that the hungry and the despised go on being ignored, hungry, and despised?

What is needed, of course, if the motivation to perform *agape* is to be increased, is for the *agape* lover to foresee some possibility for something more than sacrifice, to see some prospect of future satisfaction for himself or herself. But if heaven is taken away, what is that prospect? As we argued in the first lecture, what is needed is a prospect of paradise in this life. If it were known that *agape* could lead to an experience which is good simply to experience, then the *agape* lover might have a stronger motivation to practice *agape*.

What if Jesus' appeal to the rich young ruler had been augmented with a prognostication: If you give your wealth to the poor, you might acquire new friends and good times with those new friends. After all, when the poor would receive the young ruler's wealth, they might be enabled to stand on their feet and meet the ruler as a comrade. Might such a prognostication have enticed the young ruler to give, agapically?

Such a prognostication is realistic. The fact is that people do find it difficult to have aesthetic love, or intrinsically satisfying relationships, when they are suffering. To the extent that *agape* overcomes various forms of suffering, it does make aesthetic love more likely. Or to state it positively, to the extent that the *agape* lover gives value to the beloved, and makes the beloved stronger, to that extent the possibility of a satisfying relationship between that lover and that beloved is increased. *Agape* can be a means to aesthetic love.

But if there is that connection between *agape* and aesthetic love, and if aesthetic love is a satisfaction to experience, then the prospect of aesthetic love can serve as a motivation for the present practice of *agape*. Aesthetic love would then function as the end or goal that *agape* would strive, as a means, to reach.

What if that motivation were used to encourage *agape*? What if, for example, the Marshall Plan had been presented as an act of *agape*, but with a particular motivation? What if it had been argued that only through giving aid to those war-torn nations could their cultural life be restored, and that only with that restoration could there be a satisfying cultural community among the North Atlantic nations? That would have been using the prospect of aesthetic love as a motivation for practicing *agape*. What if it were argued that teaching does involve the short-term sacrifice of *agape*, but also the long-term satisfactions of aesthetic love? Sometimes the teacher does legitimately use an *agape* pedagogy, and sometimes the teacher, as the *agape* lover, does sacrifice. But neither is it unusual for a teacher to exercise this sacrificial love with a secret hope that, if the class goes well, an intellectual commune may develop. That secret hope could become a practical motivation.

YOUNG SEMINARIAN: You know, of course—don't you—that you have become a little incoherent?

SPEAKER: Incoherent?

YOUNG SEMINARIAN: Because you are saying that people can be motivated by the prospect of selfish gains to practice a selfless love. Those cannot be combined. Either the motivation is selfish and *agape* is lost, or *agape* is retained and the selfish motivation cannot be used.

SPEAKER: If I am incoherent here, then so is the Bible. After all, it is continually argued that if Israel loves agapically and keeps the faith with God, then Israel will be rewarded. And Jesus repeatedly affirmed that a life of love would be rewarded by entry into the Kingdom of God. Can it be that such correlations had nothing to do with motivations?

YOUNG SEMINARIAN: To me that sounds like a perverse interpretation of the Bible.

SPEAKER: Surely, if it is, it is an unintended perversity. But let me try again, on my guard against perversity.

What I have said is incoherent only if *agape* has more to do with the selfless intentions of the *agape* lover than with the effects of *agape* for the beloved. If the real meaning of *agape* is the glorification of the purity of the lover, then I am incoherent. But, surely, the Bible is not interested in the glorification of humans. So *agape* in the Bible must really be a utilitarian love, a love which seeks not to glorify the lover, but to make the lover an instrument for aiding the beloved. And, if that is the case, what's wrong with a promise of a little satisfaction for the lover, so long as that promotes *agape?* How would that depart from the old-time religion?

YOUNG SEMINARIAN: How does what you say depart from the old-time rationalization?

IV:
Solitude
and Aesthetic Love

Ladies and Gentlemen:

From the very beginning the effects of theology's odd parentage were apparent. Fathered by metaphysics and mothered by religious experience, theology has been damaged by the conflict between its parents.

Each parent sought to control the child's education. When metaphysics prevailed and religious experience was driven away from home, then religious experience was forgotten, and theology became the only academic discipline in which development was termed heresy. When religious experience prevailed, the solidity of metaphysics was forgotten, and theology became the only academic discipline in which the supremacy of enthusiasm over structure was deemed a virtue.

When the father prevailed, he tended to become tyrannical; not only did he outlaw the dynamics of religious experience, he outlawed dynamics in metaphysics itself. Metaphysical doctrines were installed as absolute; chief among them was the doctrine of causality.

Theology apparently learned about love during a period when the father prevailed. Developing its theories of love during this period, theology connected love irrevocably to causality. The orthodox theologies of

Christianity and Platonism said that the causal loves of *agape* and *eros* shall alone prevail.

This was, of course, a serious matter. People were influenced by the claims for *agape* and *eros.* But the dominance of causality created a special problem. Causality tells people that only individuals are real. Causality says that people make contact by causally affecting each other; but people who causally affect each other are separated from each other in time. The result is that the lover and the beloved stand alone, in solitude. If taken seriously, this solitude can engender a sense of tragic isolation.

That is what the tyranny of the metaphysics of causality did to theology. But this is not to say that the metaphysical father should be thrown out of the house. Metaphysics, the systematic effort to formulate generalizations of the utmost simplicity and universality, is essential to theology. Every theological notion of love must picture how people make contact with each other. At root, those pictures are metaphysical pictures: they say what the nature of being is, and how beings can make contact. A theological notion of love without a clear metaphysical foundation is merely enthusiastic; it lacks the foundation that a metaphysical picture provides. But when only those notions of love which depend on causality are accepted, then people are told that they are isolated. And that is a painful, if not a tragic, thing to be told.

It is time to call the mother home. Religious experience keeps theology informed of shifting feelings and perceptions, which are not often represented in the profundities of metaphysics. Among those feelings and perceptions is the common sense of aesthetic love. Unfortunately, religious experience is so estranged from metaphysics that the notion of aesthetic love has lost contact with metaphysics. In fact, there is no clear metaphysics appropriate to aesthetic love; there is no clear metaphysics of noncausal contact between contemporaries.

Our objective during this lecture is to welcome the mother back into the home and to get her into conversation with the father, so that a metaphysics of noncausal contact might be considered. In the ensuing hour allotted us, we can do no more than open that conversation. Our hope, nevertheless, is to do something so that theology can grow up in a home more inclined to take aesthetic love's metaphysical foundation seriously.

We hope also to stop milking this metaphor, and to turn to this audience. And we should begin by recognizing that some people—a few are in this audience—are skeptical of all metaphysical analysis. These skeptics will receive our first attention, and they deserve it. They are not ready to launch into a metaphysical analysis, because they have been too often subjected to silly metaphysical analysis. So we will attempt to stand where they stand: apart from those who are willing to dive unselfconsciously into the metaphysical depths.

Some theologians take that unselfconscious dive. They readily assume the intelligibility of language about God or of certain Christian comments, like the claim that one man's crucifixion changed all people's lives. Admittedly, other theologians refuse to take the unselfconscious dive. They usually stay away from metaphysical waters altogether, out of a fear of the linguistic undertow so commonly noted by those philosophers who pose on the beach. But the metaphysical theologians often dive into the metaphysical depths well protected by Anselm's slogan: faith seeks understanding. Anselm, a medieval realist, was confident that the ideas of faith are supported by a metaphysical substructure, and that understanding could discern that substructure.

Anselm's assumption will only annoy the skeptics. They cannot begin with the grand vision of faith; nor do they believe that understanding will reveal the metaphysical foundation for that vision. They aspire merely to understand, even if understanding is too shallow to reach the metaphysical depths. They may wish merely to know, before they die, why they were born. And many skeptics, having ventured that wish, do not expect it to be granted. They may have been repeatedly initiated into philosophical and theological schools, and now hope only to avoid the measured cadence of those who pronounce the What is What.

People skeptically inclined are not simply going to strip and dive into the metaphysical depths. They have heard voices, like the voice of Ernest Hemingway:

> What did he fear? It was not fear or dread. It was a nothing that he knew too well. It was all a nothing and a man was nothing too. It was only that and light was all it needed and a certain cleanness and order. Some lived in it and never felt it but he knew it all was nada y pues nada y nada y pues nada. Our nada who art in nada, nada be thy name thy kingdom nada thy will be nada in nada as it is in nada. Give us this nada our daily nada and nada us our nada as we nada our nadas and nada us not into nada but deliver us from nada; pues nada.[1]

People who hear such voices cannot in decency be asked simply to dive into the metaphysical depths to see

the pilings beneath a theory of aesthetic love. Sometimes theology has treated such reservations as little
more than a request for a shove. But that may not be
polite at all.

So, having stopped to consider the reluctance of those
who are skeptically inclined, where are we left? Are we
simply to drop the metaphysical question, and, in effect,
to acknowledge that noncausal commune between people cannot be examined?

That is not necessary if we are really to attempt to
stand where the skeptics stand. For not all skeptics stop
with the rejection of metaphysics. Some skeptics take
three steps more.

Admittedly, for some skeptics the abandonment of
metaphysics has no effect on how they view the world;
but for other skeptics—and it is these we are talking
about—the abandonment of metaphysics requires
three steps more.

First, for these skeptics the abandonment of metaphysics engenders a sense of cosmic solitude. For them
to abandon metaphysics is for them to admit that, for all
they know, they live in touch with nothing; it is to admit
that, for all they know, they are not in touch with something that gives some minimal meaning to everything.
It is to say, in addition, that they live with a sense of the
void that weakens actual love because it undermines
love's assumptions about how people make contact. So
the solitude the skeptics experience stems not only
from a meaningless universe but also from a debilitation
of love. The closet of metaphysical skepticism, once it
is retreated to, becomes all there really is.

Skepticism about metaphysics can lead, finally, to
what Erich Fromm refers to when he says, in a very
long sentence:

This awareness of himself as a separate entity, the awareness of his own short life span, of the fact that without his will he is born and against his will he dies, that he will die before those whom he loves, or they before him, the awareness of his aloneness and separateness, of his helplessness before the forces of nature and of society, all this makes his separate, disunited existence an unbearable prison.[2]

This step into cosmic solitude is the first step certain skeptics will take.

But there is a second step, for these skeptics are not willing to lock the door of closeted solitude— from the inside. Fromm describes this step in the sentence following that quoted a moment ago: "He would become insane could he not liberate himself from this prison and reach out, unite himself in some form or other with men, with the world outside."[3] In other words, the cosmic solitude caused by metaphysical skepticism creates a new need for love. This is paradoxical because the skepticism first weakens love by taking away the metaphysical underpinnings of love; but then it becomes apparent that a rejection of metaphysics creates a new demand for love. This is the skeptics' second step: the skeptics' solitude makes love necessary.

It is as though love once occurred in shallow water where people could stand on the bottom. But a tide of skeptical thought raised the water level, people could no longer reach the bottom, and love was terminated. Each person was alone in the waters of skepticism, and the depth of the water appeared ominous. Each person concluded that in solitude he or she might sink. So each solitary swimmer sought a new kind of contact, a new

kind of love, which could occur where the bottom remains out of reach.

Edward Albee, in *A Delicate Balance*, dramatizes the
way in which desperation about cosmic solitude can
lead one, not to reject love, but to seek love. Harry and
Edna, a couple around sixty years old, arrive at the
home of their best friends, another couple also around
sixty years old. Their arrival is not expected, and it is
met with curiosity and embarrassment. Finally, when
an explanation is sought, Harry and Edna grope to explain themselves in the following way:

> Harry: I . . . I don't know quite what happened
> then; we . . . we were . . . it was all very
> quiet, and we were all alone . . . and then
> . . . nothing happened, but . . .
> Edna: WE GOT . . . FRIGHTENED.
> Harry: We got scared.
> Edna: WE WERE . . . FRIGHTENED.
> Harry: There was nothing . . . but we were very
> scared.
> Edna: We . . . were . . . terrified.
> Harry: We were scared. It was like being lost:
> very young again, with the dark, and lost.
> There was no . . . thing . . . to be . . .
> frightened of, but . . .
> Edna: WE WERE FRIGHTENED . . . AND THERE
> WAS NOTHING.
> Harry: We couldn't stay there, and so we came
> here. You're our very best friends.
> Edna: In the whole world.[4]

Within a day it becomes apparent that they plan to
move in and stay for the indefinite future. And their
host asks them to stay, even if that means that they

bring their terror with them. In the end Harry and Edna leave, concluding, apparently, that such a love cannot be asked for or cannot be attained. But one gets the impression that such a pessimistic ending was unnecessary.

The desperation about cosmic solitude pushes one to seek love. At this second step the skeptics are still thoroughly skeptical about metaphysics, so they seek a love that can make sense without metaphysics. The skeptics seek a love that can work over a metaphysical void, without being upheld by some subsurface solidarity. This love is not like a skin stretched over the rock of faith; the love that is now needed is like a drumhead over a bottomless pit. Ordinarily, love is supported by a known metaphysical picture of how beings make contact. This new love, however, is demanded or implied by the absence of metaphysical pictures of interaction. Ordinarily one says, Love because there is a metaphysical basis for love. But at this point the skeptics are inclined to say, Love because there is no reason to love. Love is ordinarily a special implication of the metaphysical rationality of things; but this new love is the special implication of the nonrationality of things. Love's foundation is of a peculiar nature: it is a void.[5]

The skeptics need the kind of love that could provide a social solidarity, a solidarity in the present moment between contemporaries; only such a solidarity could support the individual over this void. Only such a carpet of green connections can save the skeptic from sinking into the deep blue.

At this point the skeptics are ready to take the third step. For such a social solidarity is inconceivable apart from an explanation: How is the social solidarity possible, unless one is able to be in present contact with one's contemporaries? And how is such contact possible unless one can have noncausal contact with one's contemporaries? And how is such a noncausal contact sensible, even sensible enough to act on, particularly in the Western world, apart from an explanation?

The skeptics might take a third step: in order to acquire a love capable of dealing with the cosmic solitude, the skeptics might reapproach metaphysics. The skeptics might ask the metaphysical question, How is noncausal contact with my contemporaries possible?

But it is too soon to answer this question. For there is another group, other than the skeptics, which is driven by the experience of solitude to seek a metaphysical analysis of noncausal contact between contemporaries. This group is comprised of metaphysicians who themselves are left strangely alone; and they need a metaphysical analysis that can help to replace solitude with sociality.

Until the advent of relativity in historical study and in physics and in the social sciences, the metaphysicians thought that their communication was sustained by a constant language. Then the relativists came along and said: "You can still send words to each other; but that is of no use anymore. The words change meaning from moment to moment." And the metaphysicians rose up and asked, "Why do the words change meaning from moment to moment?" And the relativists said, "The words change meaning because the words refer to things and persons, and the things and persons change from moment to moment. So you are out of touch." A quick look at recent philosophy is required if we are to understand why it was the relativists who broke the news, and what it was that the relativists were saying.

Philosophically speaking, what happened was this. Relations had always been conceived causally. But causality did not put people out of touch until the old metaphysics of substance philosophy was replaced by the new metaphysics of process philosophy.

Until around a hundred years ago substance philosophy was the mainstream of philosophical thought in the Western world. Substance philosophy affirmed that persons and things, in their deepest sense, do not change, so the words which refer to them do not change. It said that what was most real about anything was some idea, or essence, or form, which in-formed or guided that thing, and was eternal and unchanging. Whatever change there was in a person or a thing was superficial and unimportant. Whether Plato or Aristotle or any of their philosophical children were speaking, there was a common meaning when they said: Fulfill yourself. There was some constant human nature which was real, though not perfectly actualized in practice, and one was admonished to bring that nature from its status as an ideal potentiality to the status of an actuality. Maturation should be the process through which one becomes, or realizes in practice, one's ideal and unchanging nature; this is the root of the easy phrase: self-realization. In many ways we continue to subscribe to substance philosophy: We still strive to make the United States live up to its true nature, as that is stated in the Constitution and the Declaration of Independence. Most theories of equal justice assume that each person has an innate potentiality and deserves the opportunity to become who he or she is. Every time a discovery is made in science, it is not thought that nature has changed, but that the scientific community has changed—an eternal reality has moved from not being understood to being understood.

In each of these processes, it is assumed that what is most real about the thing is its essence, and essences endure unchanged through time. So the words do not change, because they refer to a reality that remains constant through time.

With substance philosophy, causality does not isolate people from each other. Certainly, causal relations take time, and that means that one always relates causally to someone in one's past or one's future, and never to someone in one's literal present. But this temporal gap is no problem in substance philosophy, because the past person endures essentially unchanged into the present. So to know the past person is really to know the present person, and to know a person is to be in relation with that person.

So the Jane in Alice's literal present is not really unknown. Jane, according to substance philosophy, will be the same Jane until her dying day. To know the past Jane is really to know the present Jane even though no information from the present Jane is received. Jane endures essentially unchanged—except for some accidental, contingent and superficial changes Jane may suffer. The word "Jane" is unchanging because it refers to the same, essentially unchanging person.

This means that when causality was combined with substance philosophy, solitude was not a problem. Alice, for all intents and purposes, could relate to Jane in the present moment.

But, then, relativity undercut substance philosophy. Substance philosophy had said that a thing is what it is

primarily for internal reasons; a thing's own essence is its dominating principle and supplies its aim. Relativity argued the converse: a thing is what it is primarily for external reasons; a thing's own internal nature is largely the result of influence from other things in the past. But from moment to moment, as each new present moves into the past, the past changes; that is, the things in the past change. And as they change, what they give to the present changes. This means that the present changes, because the internal nature of the present is largely the result of past influences. In fact, this process of change is so thorough, it is more accurate to think of the present thing as just a momentary reality, a phase in an ongoing process.

In the twentieth century, process philosophy accepted relativity and argued that what is most real is not permanence, but movement. To a large extent the metaphysics of process philosophy replaced the metaphysics of substance philosophy, and what was thought to be most real was the dynamic becoming of things, rather than the static essence, or being, of things. With process philosophy persons and things change; so the words change. And when causality was combined with process philosophy, solitude became a real problem. Alice was then alone.

The effects of process philosophy may not be believable if it is not understood that to assert the predominance of process is to make a radical assertion. The assertion even plays havoc with our language. With process philosophy it is not really proper to speak of a person or a thing as undergoing change. If there is no enduring core to an entity, if reality in its deepest sense is a fluidity rather than a stability, then there is no continu-

ing person or thing, no noun which is through time the subject receiving the effects of change. Rather, the subject is a verb. The person or the thing is a verbal reality; the process which each is, is what each is. And what each reality is, is only a momentary phenomenon. It is, after all, not substances but relations which internally determine what is. And from moment to moment these relations change and, in turn, change what is.

As a consequence, Jane is a momentary process that has just arisen and is soon to perish. The Jane of this moment is not the Jane of a moment ago or the Jane of a moment from now. The meaning of the word "Jane" changes, because it refers to a new person each moment.

Solitude is the consequence. At least that is the consequence when process philosophy is conjoined with causality so closely that causal relations are the only means whereby people can have access to each other. Causality dictates that, quite literally, Alice can receive information only from the Jane of the past—it takes time for anything to be causally transmitted. According to causality, Alice simply cannot know the Jane of the present moment. This literal ignorance of the Jane of the present moment is not a serious problem with substance philosophy because, for all intents and purposes, Alice does know the real Jane, even the Jane of the present moment, because the Jane of the past is known and, through time, the real Jane remains essentially the same. But with process philosophy this literal ignorance is a real problem, because Jane is a process. The Jane of this moment is a new and different Jane from the Jane of a moment ago. The Jane of a moment ago has perished and the Jane of this moment is the actual Jane. But

Alice does not know the actual Jane of this moment. Nor does Alice know any person or thing of this moment.

Alice is all alone now. And Alice can well begin to have the kinds of foreboding had by the skeptics. That can happen even though Alice is not a skeptic, even though Alice still believes in metaphysical speculation. For metaphysics itself has led Alice to the realization of her solitude in the present moment. But if Alice cannot settle for solitude, she needs social commune.

There is a curious closing of the circle here. Process philosophy has received the tradition of substance philosophy, with its claim for the primacy of a static being over a dynamic becoming; and process philosophy has rejected that and argued for the primacy of becoming over being. However, this primacy of becoming has so isolated the contemporary individual that that individual must seek a new form of static being— the social being of the present moment. The individual, to overcome the solitude caused by flux, must seek in the stasis of the present moment a social being. There is a momentary pause in becoming, a pause which occurs in the present moment; and in that pause a social reality, a social being, is sought.

This raises a metaphysical question: Can there be, in addition to causal relations, a noncausal contact between contemporaries? If such contact cannot be metaphysically explained, then solitude is more comprehensible than togetherness, and talk about being together with others becomes problematic.

But before we offer our comments on metaphysics and noncausality, we should ask if there are any questions about what has been said.

(A period of silence.)

THE SAME YOUNG SEMINARIAN: I hope you noticed that I waited before I raised my hand.

SPEAKER: I did notice that and commend you for your courtesy.

YOUNG SEMINARIAN: But no one else asked to speak.

SPEAKER: Again, I would concede your point, and would ask you not to apologize for asking too large a proportion of the questions. Remember, with each passing minute, with the departure of each additional member of the audience, you constitute an ever larger proportion of those assembled here.

YOUNG SEMINARIAN: You keep saying that we will be stuck with solitude if we don't move on to metaphysical analysis. But I am beginning to have doubts.

SPEAKER: What doubts?

YOUNG SEMINARIAN: The solitude seems trivial to me. In fact, no one—not even a solitary astronaut on the moon—is separated from anyone else by more than a little over a second—given, that is, proper instruments for communication. But you are saying that solitude is significant. You are saying, for example, that I am significantly isolated from you because of that inconceivably small split second it takes my voice to travel the few feet which separate me from you. Is it this solitude which is so dreadful? Haven't you exaggerated what is, in the last analysis, an utterly insignificant temporal gap? Is fear of this solitude to prompt us to follow you into what you continue to call "the metaphysical depths"?

SPEAKER: You are a harsh critic. But give me a chance to explain myself. Will you concede that, technically, I am right? That if causality and process philosophy are combined, the self is literally isolated from all other actual persons, from all those who stand in the self's own split-second, quantum slice of time.

YOUNG SEMINARIAN: I never denied it. I merely argued that that quantum slice of time, as you choose to call it, is so small that it really does not make for a significant isolation.

SPEAKER: You continue to add the adjective "significant," and to say that there is no "significant" isolation. I take it that since you acknowledge that the isolation is literally true, your argument has to do with its significance.

YOUNG SEMINARIAN: You have heard me correctly.

SPEAKER: Fine. I would argue only with your ability to interpret the influence of metaphysical models. You are saying that the causal model is not influential enough to create significant isolation; and I am saying that it is. But you have underrated the influence of metaphysical models. Throughout history people have not treated models as trivial but as highly influential in the determination of what is or is not significant.

YOUNG SEMINARIAN: But are minute quantities, like split seconds, highly influential?

SPEAKER: Lucretius thought so. He invented his atomic theory to lessen people's fear of death; and yet Lucretius' atoms were so small they could not be seen. Newton used a mechanical model of nature, and his contemporaries might not have expected that model to affect human personality. Yet, without placing responsibility on Newton, it can be said that mechanistic models have contributed to a significant dehumanization of Western society. We argued in the first lecture that *agape* and *eros*, depending as they do on a model of causality, may have fostered significant imperialistic and exploitative attitudes.

I have just attempted to show how academic metaphysics can drive one to the conclusion that he or she is significantly isolated. We have set forth a model that combines causality and process. Our contention is that this model can and does have something to do with people's sense of life as fleeting and unstable. This may be reflected in everything from "future shock" to the bumper sticker I recently saw, which read, FIGHT ENTROPY. And this instability can induce feelings of solitariness. Those feelings cannot be eliminated by a removal of the metaphysical model, because, as you have acknowledged, the model is literally correct.

YOUNG SEMINARIAN: You have certainly moved. You may have started by standing where those who are skeptical of metaphysics stand. Now you are shoulder to shoulder with the metaphysicians. But, please, go on with your lecture.

Thank you. Let me begin with a difficult admission: to explain noncausal relations between contemporaries seems to require the introduction of God. Certainly, in one sense, that is to admit a failure of thought; it is reminiscent of the *deus ex machina*. But if the introduction of God makes a theory reprehensible, then the theories of *agape* and *eros* are equally reprehensible, for they require God in order to explain their metaphysics of causal interaction. The theorists of *agape* were left with the question, What enables the lover to give? And it was answered, God must be the efficient cause, giving love to the lover, who is, consequently, enabled to give love to the beloved. The theorists of *eros* were left with the question, What enables the beloved to be so alluring to the lover? And it was answered, God must be the final cause of the beloved's allure, giving the beloved the attractiveness that lures the lover into action.[6] In both instances a causal action between persons had to be explained; in both instances it was concluded that reference to the lover and the beloved alone was insufficient to explain the causal relatedness. And in both instances it was concluded that God's causal action must be included in the explanation.

For the same reason we must introduce God to explain noncausal relatedness: reference to the human parties to the love seems insufficient.

Martin Buber and Paul Tillich also looked at a love which we have argued is analogous to aesthetic love and concluded that the mystical presence of God must be introduced. Buber explains the I-You relationship by proposing that "the mediatorship of this You of all beings" makes possible our relationship to all beings. He contends that the contribution of this "You of all beings," or God, is indispensable to an adequate understanding of the I-You relationship. So Buber will say: "Actually, we receive what we did not have before, in such a manner that we know: it has been given to us. In the language of the Bible: 'Those who wait for God will receive strength in exchange.' "[7]

Paul Tillich acknowledges that the reunion of separated beings occurs only when those beings are "taken into" the Spiritual Presence. Separate human beings do not have in themselves the capacity to reunite with those others with whom they should reunite; this inability is due not only to their finitude, or their lack of power, but also to their sin, which magnifies the natural separation between persons into what Tillich calls "estrangement." So Tillich will say that the existential and "ambiguous life is raised above itself to a transcendence that it could not achieve by its own power."[8] Certainly, the lovers also contribute something to the love; but the presence of God is needed to make the love possible.

Similarly, the existence of aesthetic love might argue for a mystical presence, which comes between contemporaries and brings them into an immediate and noncausal relatedness. The evidence supporting that argument may be limited to what common practice and common sense tell us.

When people are joined in certain bonds of relatedness, their bonds of relatedness seem quantitatively larger than the sum of their separate contributions would indicate. There is, in short, a synergistic phenomenon. Individuals come together and they each have capacities for contributing to a relationship. But when they are actually together, they are united by bonds which have a power greater than the sum of their separate capacities for bondedness. It is as though there is "something more" which contributes to the strength of the bondedness.

It is our contention that "something more" provides a spiritual medium between people, making noncausal contact possible. This contention, which concurs with comments by Buber and Tillich, might provide the beginnings for a metaphysical explanation of noncausal contact between contemporaries. This is to say that people might be together in the present moment because they exist together in an atmosphere of communion, an atmosphere for which they are not entirely responsible. If this metaphysical suggestion were accurate, then aesthetic love would not be a love stretched over a metaphysical void.

In addition, when some people recognize that the love between them is greater than what they could have made, they react with gratitude. It seems inappropriate to react with pride, as though the love were entirely their own accomplishment. Nor does the synergistic quality of the love seem merely serendipitous. Gratitude acknowledges that there is something about the universe which facilitates an escape from painful solitude. Gratitude expresses the conviction that the universe, in some respect, warrants gratitude.

There is, in modern physics, a puzzle about how the nucleus of an atom holds together. The major components of the nucleus, the protons and the neutrons, should fly apart. The protons are positively charged and would normally repel each other because they have the same (positive) charge, and the neutrons, because they have no charge, would not inhibit that normal repulsion. However, the nuclear particles, including the protons and the neutrons, are—despite the repulsion— bound together in the nucleus by the strongest force in nature, the field of strong interaction. H. Yukawa suggested in 1935 that the field of strong interaction was created by a meson, the nuclear exchange particle.

The exchange particle can be thought of as binding the nuclear particles in a relatedness of the present moment, but in such a way that none of those entities causally acts on the other. This field of strong interaction may be thought of as analogous to aesthetic love: both exemplify a noncausal relatedness among contemporary entities.[9]

And the meson, the nuclear exchange particle, may

be thought of as analogous to God. However, it has never been observed creating a field of strong interaction. (It is assumed that efforts at observation have been unsuccessful because the life of the meson is too brief for observation.) The existence of the field is known. The existence of the exchange particle is merely postulated. It has been postulated because there is no other apparent explanation for the existence of the field of strong interaction than the existence of "something more," which makes the field possible.

Something analogous to the field of strong interaction can be seen in the rare phenomenon of love between enemies. Those enemies may be military or political enemies, but they may also be personal enemies—for example, a neighbor or the person who works next to you. On occasion such natural enemies sit down together and are able not only to work together or be kind to each other, but to enjoy a genuine bondedness that grows between them. It is strange when this happens, for enemies have for each other a natural repulsion. Yet love between enemies is a bondedness which is sufficiently strong to overcome that natural repulsion. That bondedness cannot be explained sheerly by reference to the contributions of the enemies; the strength of that bondedness is greater than the sum of the potentials for bondedness contributed by the enemies. The bonds do not seem capable of explanation, except by the contribution from "something more," something analogous to the exchange particle.

Jesus may have referred to love for enemies as an example of *agape*, and love for enemies may perfectly exemplify *agape* because it is a gift to the unlovable. But when love for enemies becomes love between enemies something new occurs. The causal relatedness of *agape*—from God, to the lover, to the beloved—is replaced by a mutual bondedness between the enemies in the present moment. A classical, causal model of relations is replaced by a modern, field-theory model of relations. When this happens, a relatedness occurs which requires, for its explanation, the introduction of "something more."

Speaking theoretically, we might call that bondedness between enemies aesthetic love. We might think of that bondedness as resulting from a mystical presence, "something more" than what the lovers contribute. We have not identified what that "something more" is; but we have called it God.

Addendum

(Note: Due to lengthy questioning from the audience, a portion of the preceding lecture had to be omitted. I chose to omit the following pages because they were least intelligible to a general audience. They may, in fact, be suited only for someone who has done previous study in the philosophy of Alfred North Whitehead.)

We have issued some sweeping generalizations about process philosophy and have not documented them. We said that when process philosophy replaced permanence with process the individual was more fundamentally isolated by causality than had been the case when permanence was thought to prevail. But we have not supported that claim by reference to any process philosopher. We will attempt for a few moments to do just that, by referring to the preeminent process philosopher, Alfred North Whitehead.

Whitehead's appreciation of the importance of process is obvious; he says:

> Without doubt, if we are to go back to that ultimate, integral experience, unwarped by the sophistications of theory, that experience whose elucidation is the final aim of philosophy, the flux of things is one ultimate generalization around which we must weave our philosophical system.[10]

> The actual world is a process, and that process is the becoming of actual entities.[11]

There are two species of process, however: First, there is the macroscopic process, where all the things in the past world contribute the fundamental conditions for the development of a new thing in the present moment. Second, there is the microscopic process, whereby that new thing develops internally, from a mere set of conditions for existence to the realization of a definite actuality.[12] There are two kinds of causality, correlative to each species of process: first, the macroscopic process works by efficient causation, whereby the qualities of the past things are transmitted to provide conditions for the present things; second, the microscopic process works by final causation, whereby the aim, or goal, of the new thing determines, within its limits, what it shall be.[13]

These notions can be illustrated by reference to Jane, to whom we referred earlier. Jane is a microscopic process of the present moment, guided in part by Jane's momentary aim for herself. In each new moment there is a new Jane, who may closely resemble the old Jane, but, who is, nevertheless, new. She is a new Jane because the things of the past world, which provide the conditions for the Jane of the present moment, are things which themselves have changed. They transmit through the efficient causation of the macroscopic process new conditions within which the final causation of the new Jane must work. Relativity is finally responsible for the changeableness of that series of events we call Jane: relations between the past things and the Jane of the present moment internally determine, in part, what the new Jane can be.

This efficient causation of the macroscopic process is the only means through which things or people can relate. Jane can be for Alice only an efficient cause in Alice's past. But Jane and Alice as they actually are, in the literal present, are out of touch.

Whitehead knows that people think they are in contact with their literal contemporaries, and he says that that conviction results from looking at the potentiality of some past thing to be something in the present, and thinking of that as what some present actuality is. But, in fact, the present actualities cannot be known, because they cannot affect each other. Whitehead can say, then, that "so far as physical relations are concerned, contemporary events happen in *causal* independence of each other."[14] Of course, it appears that we are in contact with a strictly contemporary world, an extensive continuum stretching before us in the literal present. But this is an illusion, caused by what Whitehead calls "presentational immediacy." What we actually are in contact with is the past world presented to our senses. This past world is, with regard to the present world, no more than a set of potentialities for what might happen in the present, actual world. But in the actual, present world free choices are being exercised, and no one, except Jane, knows what those present choices are when they are made. So the apparent presentness of the world is really only a set of potentialities from the past for what might happen in the present. The actual present world is "incurably atomic"; it is comprised of discontinuous and independent events.

Whitehead's philosophy, because it includes doctrines of process and of efficient causation (as the only way in which entities can relate), allows for no actual social commune between literal contemporaries. Isolation in the present world, which is the only actual world there is, is the human being's fate.[15]

Of course, this interpretation of Whitehead could be disparaged as a quibble over the split second that separates the present person from the past actual world. But it was Whitehead who asked us to concentrate on the single unit of experience; that present atomic occasion of experience was his metaphysical model. And from the perspective of that unit, the split-second separation is significant. Whitehead is the one who, in effect, said, Test me by whether I can explain the world by reference to that indivisibly small unit of experience. Whitehead asked us to look at subjective experience: "Finally, the reformed subjectivist principle must be repeated: that apart from the experiences of subjects there is nothing, nothing, nothing, bare nothingness."[16] But the experience looked at is the subjective experience of the indivisibly small actual entity. Reference to this entity provides the data for all that is said. "This ontological principle means that actual entities are the only *reasons;* so that to search for a *reason* is to search for one or more actual entities."[17] So there can be no "reasons" for a social reality between entities;[18] reasons and the word "reality" refer only to the experiences of individual entities themselves.

In summary, according to Whitehead's metaphysics, the sense of contact with contemporaries is mere appearance, mere potentiality. The actual entity is isolated from its actual contemporary world. It is quite appropriate to draw from this metaphysical model the most profound implications about the individual isolation of the actual entity. The present actual occasions of experience are all that is actual, and each such occasion is shut off from all other actual occasions—or from the only actual world there is.[19]

V:
Boredom and Aesthetic Love

Ladies and Gentlemen:

Some people with a worldly wisdom may nod when we attempt to indicate one by one the inadequacies of *agape* and *eros* and mutual love. And they may smile benignly when we point out the problems with philosophies of substance and process. Over the years they may have grown suspicious of large claims about love. So when we assert that aesthetic love brings satisfaction, they may look down and pick their fingernails.

A few of the wise may be here, even in this audience. They may realize that those of us who are common and who consult common sense may badly need to believe that the experience of aesthetic love is a satisfying experience, in and of itself. They may know that that quality of satisfaction is the keystone in that arch which we are seeking to build over the flux and the solitude it brings. They may know that for us the escape from the flux and the solitude is fruitless if aesthetic love is not aesthetically valuable. After all, if aesthetic love is not valuable, it is boring. And what is the point of replacing the isolation of solitude with the tedium of social bonds? The wise may know that whether aesthetic love is an escape from solitude, or whether it is not, is finally of no consequence. For they may know that being with others is, in the last analysis, a bore. But the wise may also know how damaging it would be to say this out loud. So they may choose to remain silent.

They may be keeping mum for the same reason that a potential spoilsport[1] might keep mum. The spoilsport interprets what is sport for others as unnecessary or false or pernicious. However, the spoilsport knows that to speak of this may break the spell and ruin the sport. The spoilsport knows that not even the cheat is so dangerous, for the cheat at least accepts the illusion. Spoilsports who are conscientious objectors are sometimes jailed; spoilsports who say "Humbug" at Christmas are sometimes not invited. But some potential spoilsports refuse to become actual spoilsports. Out of cowardice or consideration, they may not want to make trouble for others. And those potential spoilsports may keep mum. They may come to watch, and nod in assent whenever possible, and pick their fingernails when necessary— and keep mum. And the wise may be just like those potential spoilsports.

Now, of course, we have no evidence that the wise are keeping mum. If they are keeping mum, they must keep mum about keeping mum, or they are not really keeping mum at all.

What can we do then? What can we do but hurl into that silent presence what reasons there may be for thinking that there is satisfaction in the experience of aesthetic love, knowing all along that these reasons may be received with even further silence and a further picking of the fingernails?

Certainly, this is a gamble. How can the satisfaction acquired from aesthetic love be proved, any more than the humor of a joke can be proved? How can we hope to overturn the pessimism of those who are keeping mum—if they are keeping mum? How, except with a certain luck? But if that be gambling, so may every other theological proposal be. (And this consideration of the value of aesthetic love is a theological proposal.)

Albert Camus chooses to imagine Sisyphus happy,[2] and that may be an apt choice. But if Sisyphus were a theologian, he should be imagined another way: walking back down the hill, with a distracted gait and a contorted mouth, as the inveterate gambler, figuring his odds on the next rock.

However, before we begin our gamble on this last rock, we should pause at the bottom of the hill to state more fully our reason for responding to the wise. When by their silence the wise imply that aesthetic love is not a satisfaction to experience, they imply that aesthetic love is really not a love for before the fall; a love that cannot provide satisfying experience is not the love appropriate to the good life. In fact, the wise imply that aesthetic love is worthless; aesthetic love was not introduced for its utility, and they believe it has no nonutilitarian, or intrinsic, value. So the wise are left with only love after the fall; in their relations with others they can do no more than attempt to work against the negativities of life; there is no possibility of a positive love. In their life with others the wise can anticipate no more than a struggle to overcome failure. In one's only life, that may be a desperate anticipation.

To make matters worse, they have lost more than a love for before the fall. Even their love after the fall, even *agape* and *eros,* are to an extent undermined. We have noted earlier that the life before the fall functions as the end for the life after the fall. Aesthetic love may be only one aspect of the life before the fall; but if aesthetic love is nullified, then the end, which is the life before the fall, is partly nullified. *Agape* and *eros*, as means to that end, are called into question. It should be noted, however, that aesthetic love is only the social aspect of the life before the fall. There may be, in addition, an individual aspect to the life before the fall. So *agape* and *eros* may still foster aesthetic phenomena that are individual.[3]

The fact remains that the wise are in a predicament, and this lecture will seek to help them out. Our objective will be to describe for them how aesthetic love is aesthetically valuable. To phrase our question in a relevant manner, What is there about the relatedness among us, those of us remaining—we happy few—in this lecture hall, here and now, which is valuable simply for being experienced? Is there some quality to our present relatedness which is in itself valuable? Can that quality be described aesthetically?

We must begin by recognizing again a few of those distinctions crucial to any consideration of aesthetic love. Aesthetic love is characterized by nonindividuality, noncausality, and nontemporality, while conventional aesthetic theory, like the conventional loves, is characterized by individuality, causality, and temporality.

According to most aesthetic theory there is the thing beheld, or the aesthetic object, and there is the beholder, or the aesthetic subject. The aesthetic object causally affects the aesthetic subject, inducing an aesthetic experience. The aesthetic object has aesthetic value and some expression of that value is causally transmitted by means of light waves, or sound waves, to the aesthetic subject. Because the aesthetic object and the aesthetic subject are causally related, they are also temporally related. According to the causal model, the subject receives a message that was released from the object slightly earlier.

We speak of how an orchestra is heard by an audience. The orchestra's performance is an aesthetic object, and that performance is causally transmitted, by means of sound waves, to an audience that sits at a distance from the orchestra. The orchestra's performance is interpreted as an object on display, suitable for analysis; the audience has a subjective experience of that object.

But the aesthetic characteristics of aesthetic love are different. Here, it is as though we were asking, What is the orchestral sound for the violinist, while the violinist is playing and contributing to that sound? And here we are not talking about the violinist as a close-range analyst of the orchestral sound, but about the violinist as an involved participant, caught up in the sweep of the music. For the violinist so involved, the subject-object distinction is broken; the observer is part of the observed. There is no aesthetic object, set up and away, on display, suitable for analysis; and there is no detached, observing subject. Nor is the relationship between the orchestra and the violinist a causal and temporal relationship. The violinist is not principally concerned with hearing the previous note, and then reacting to it. The violinist and the orchestra are noncausally together in the present moment, contributing to a common sound.

For an aesthetics of aesthetic love the conventional characteristics of individuality (separated objects and subjects), causality and temporality, are replaced by nonindividuality, noncausality and nontemporality.

The aesthetic lover does not function as a detached subject analyzing the objective aesthetic love; the aesthetic lover is involved in the aesthetic love in such a way that the subject-object distinction is blurred. However, the nonindividuality, or sociality, in aesthetic love has limits. In the second lecture, when talking of the mystical roots of aesthetic love, we noted that the roots of aesthetic love are not those of Eastern mysticism, with its goal of total union of the self with the holy other and the consequent loss of identity. Aesthetic love follows the less extreme form of nonindividuality, which is the communion where the identity of the self is retained. Consequently, in an aesthetics of aesthetic love, while the subject-object distinction is blurred and the observer becomes part of the observed, private and public aesthetic qualities remain. The public aesthetic quality resides in the social relatedness of aesthetic love, the relatedness among the aesthetic lovers. The private aesthetic experience of that public quality occurs in the lover, who is, at the same time, a participant in that aesthetic love.

Equally, an aesthetics of aesthetic love is characterized by noncausality and nontemporality. The aesthetic lover's private aesthetic experience is not causally separated from the public aesthetic quality. The experience and the experienced, the private and the public, the lover and the love are noncausally together. And, as noncausally together, they are also nontemporally together in the present moment.

Aesthetic love is valuable because it is intrinsically valuable. This too is analogous to the violinist. For the violinist the confluence of sounds, which constitute the orchestral sound, is appreciated as the public relatedness between that violinist and other members of the orchestra; and that public relatedness has a quality, the experience of which, in the privacy of the violinist's experience, is intrinsically satisfying.

This may be strange talk, but it has precedents. Some aestheticians have rejected the subject-object distinction by reverting to a quasi-mystical epistemology which was prevalent in the ancient world. This epistemology, this way of knowing, is expressed in the special meaning of *gnosis:* knowledge of the participator, which may be realized in mystical communion or in particular activities, such as sexual union. *Gnosis* is distinguished from the knowledge of the spectator, which results from analytic and synthetic research.[4] F. David Martin, in *Art and the Religious Experience*, distinguishes a spectator from a participator:

> The spectator remains clearly conscious of himself as distinct from the aesthetic object, whereas the participator becomes so absorbed in receiving and retaining the aesthetic object that in this profound intimacy he tends to lose any sense of subject-object duality.[5]

In the participative experience, according to Martin,

> the "concrete suchness" of the object penetrates and permeates the participator's consciousness to the point that consciousness loses almost all of its self-consciousness, until there is nothing but the object. The subjective side of experience "becomes" the object, the subjective and objective poles of experience melting into a unitary phenomenon.[6]

Martin, however, goes farther than we would. He seems to obliterate the subject-object distinction, while we would retain it in a weak form, in which a public-private distinction is still meaningful.

But it is time to raise again the question of boredom. If we are ever to make the mum speak, we must move beyond the preliminaries and say what there is about aesthetic love which is aesthetically valuable.

Aesthetic love is a relatedness, a social reality, with a positive quality. Formally, the quality is that of being interesting, and its opposite is that of being boring. Aesthetic value is necessarily interesting; to speak of an uninteresting aesthetic phenomenon is to utter a contradiction. And if aesthetic value is positive value, its opposite is not some evil, some negativity that must be negated. Its opposite is an absence of interestingness; it is the state of being boring.

Specifically, the aesthetic quality is the peculiar tension that arises in the bondedness conjoining diverse people. The presence of that tension is what makes aesthetic love interesting. The optimal tension is comparable to an optimal tension of a spring holding two movable objects together. If the objects move too far apart, the spring is sprung; it becomes more like a straight wire; its springiness, which is its life, is lost. If the objects move too close together, the spring goes slack, and its springiness is lost in the alternative way. The optimal tension is reached at that point where further movement apart would make the spring go taut.

Aesthetic lovers are like the objects connected by the spring. When the lovers are optimally diverse, the spring is optimally alive. When the spring is optimally alive, the lovers have the fullest experience of the tension in the spring. But when the lovers are either too remote from each other or too close to each other, the spring goes taut or slack. The spring loses its life, and the lovers lose the experience of that life.

There are, then, two ways in which aesthetic love can fail to be interesting. People can be so remote from each other that the tension in their conjunction is lost; here, remoteness overwhelms tension. At the other extreme people can be so close to each other that the tension in their conjunction is lost; here, closeness overwhelms tension.

Remoteness and closeness are terms that refer to the absence of a quality of relatedness. Remoteness refers to the absence of a quality that might make a live conjunction, even with extreme differences among people. Closeness refers to the absence of a quality that might make a live conjunction, even with extreme similarities among people.

We could proceed immediately to discuss formal aesthetics and describe other "diversity-within-conjunction" characterizations of aesthetic value. But, rather than do that now, we will first illustrate this characterization of aesthetic value in love.

Jesus made two very odd comments about love, and each illustrates one way in which aesthetic love's tension may be induced. Jesus said, "You have heard that it was said, 'You shall love your neighbor and hate your enemy.' But I say to you, Love your enemies and pray for those who persecute you." (Matt. 5:43–44.) Whatever Jesus intended by this saying, it remains true that the love of enemies does function to induce a particular tension in aesthetic love. Aesthetic love can fail when people become so remote from each other that their conjunctions are taut; they do not hear each other, they speak past each other, or they hate each other. Jesus cited the tradition in which it was said that enemies should hate each other, and hatred does represent the absence of a quality of relatedness that permits enemies to relate, despite their differences. With hatred, remoteness overwhelms tension. However, the doctrine that there should be love between enemies says that there should be a live conjunction, despite the differences which separate people. When love between enemies does arise, that conjunction obviously embodies tension, and the enemies experience that tension, and they may find it aesthetically satisfying.

Similarly when politics conjoins people with extreme differences, it creates a tension that overcomes remoteness. Political wars are a case of remoteness overwhelming tension. But when political wars are put down and political machinery is made to work, that functioning of politics may be aesthetically valuable. Politics, in a bare-bones sense, is something more dramatic than the art of the possible. It is the art of getting enemies to work together, whether it be in a local campaign or in international diplomacy. When enemies work together, there is a live conjunction, despite the differences that separate them. And that conjunction embodies tension and inspires a sense of tension in the participants, which may be aesthetically satisfying.

Jesus commented on another kind of relationship. This relationship certainly was not ethical, and on the surface it did not seem even to be a loving relationship. But on closer examination it seems to be an instance of a live conjunction as an alternative to extreme closeness among people. Two days before the Passover a woman anointed Jesus' head with very expensive ointment and the disciples objected, saying, "Why this waste? For this ointment might have been sold for a large sum, and given to the poor." (Matt. 26:8–9.) Who can dispute with the disciples on ethical grounds? If the primary consideration is to deal with the evils of life, then morality is clearly supreme, and they have suggested the moral—in this case, the agapic—response. But Jesus, at that moment, may not have been primarily concerned with the evils of life. Just then he seemed to be primarily concerned with the positive character of what little immediate experience remained to him. And he said, "Why do you trouble the woman? For she has done a beautiful thing to me. For you always have the poor with you, but you will not always have me." (Matt. 26:10–11.) Jesus' comment emphasized the difference between the poor and himself as potential participants in a loving relation: the poor would be around always and Jesus was soon to die. Given that way of describing the potential participants in a loving relation, one would tend to choose to be related to the one who was soon to die. There is something casual in one's relatedness with people who are healthy and seem destined to live many years longer; but there is something poignant in one's relatedness with one who will die within a few days. It seems apparent that one is attracted to relations with people who are different from oneself; and, usually, the relation with one who is soon to die is a relation with one different from oneself. Jesus' comment can be interpreted to point to such a relation, and to say that the relation between more diverse people (ordinary people and one soon to die) is sometimes more valuable than the relation between more similar people.

In other words, the story of the anointment can serve

to illustrate how greater diversity in a conjunction can increase the value of that conjunction. Also, it can serve to illustrate that an aesthetically powerful love should at times take precedence over an ethically important love. While Jesus' comment on love between enemies can illustrate that aesthetic tension can be increased by overcoming remoteness, the comment on the anointment can illustrate that aesthetic tension can be increased by overcoming closeness.

The second point can be illustrated by a comment on marriage. A marital relationship can fail because the spouses are related in such a way that their differences are obscured. Their relatedness is slack, routinized, and monotonous. Closeness has overwhelmed tension, and boredom is the result. If the aesthetic tension of the marital conjunction is to be increased, it would seem that the closeness should be replaced by greater diversity. Something must be done about the marriage so that differences between the spouses are better appreciated through new forms of relatedness.

Again, none of this is to say that Jesus had in mind some notion of the aesthetic value of love. It is merely to say that Western civilization has found itself appreciating love as Jesus portrayed it. And it is to suggest that sometimes our appreciation may be attributed to love's aesthetic value, rather than to its ethical value.

There may be a similar appreciation of the aesthetic value of love implicit in certain modern comments on love. Paul Tillich does not talk of the aesthetic value of love. However, the movement of people from separation to reunion requires elements of diversity as well as similarity. Love requires separation, or diversity; so love is nullified the moment all separation is lost in the attainment of total reunion. "Fulfilled love is, at the same time, extreme happiness and the end of happiness. The separation is overcome. But without the separation there is no love and no life."[7] What Tillich calls "happiness" seems to correspond to what we have called aesthetic satisfaction. So the preceding quotation says, in our terms, that when closeness overwhelms tension, the aesthetic value of love is lost. Corresponding to our claim that the optimally interesting love conjoins the greatest diversity possible within a conjunction, Tillich seems to argue that the greater the separation overcome, the greater the love. He says, "Love manifests its greatest power there where it overcomes the greatest separation."[8]

The combination of diversity and conjunction is implicit also in Denis de Rougemont's classic study of romantic love, *Love in the Western World*. De Rougemont, like Tillich, does not claim to be analyzing an aesthetic love; in fact, he says he is discussing a version of *eros*. Nevertheless, aesthetic characteristics are implicit in the answer to the principal question he asks himself. De Rougemont's study centers around the legend of Tristan and Iseult, and at one point de Rougemont asks, What is the legend of Tristan and Iseult really about? He concludes that it is about obstacles, which keep the lovers apart from each other. The obstacles range from Iseult's jealous husband, who tries to keep the two apart, to the naked sword, which lies between Tristan and Iseult when they—literally—sleep together. De Rougemont says that the obstructions "foster love" and make the love valuable "for its own sake."[9] It seems that the obstacles function to keep the lovers sufficiently apart from each other that they can still yearn for each other. In our language, the obstacles seem to increase the diversity of the lovers, and to heighten the tension of the love. The result is that the love is valuable "for its own sake," or aesthetically valuable; it is so valuable as an end in itself that people will give even their lives to experience it.[10]

These, then, are some Biblical comments and some modern comments that can be interpreted as aesthetic comments about love. They have been interpreted as aesthetic comments because implicit in them are indications of diversity within conjunction. It might still be asked, however, whether there are explicit and formal elaborations of the notion that aesthetic value can be defined by reference to diversity within conjunction. Rather than attempt to make a systematic survey of all such theories, we will describe only a few, choosing those which seem particularly relevant to our earlier remarks.

Alfred North Whitehead said, "All aesthetic experience is feeling arising out of the realization of contrast under identity."[11] Elsewhere he refers to width and unity[12] and width and narrowness.[13] "Contrast" and "width" refer to the degree to which the qualities of the related factors stand apart from each other, and "identity," "unity," and "narrowness" refer to the degree to which their qualities have real potentiality for standing together. These terms correspond, then, to what we have called diversity and conjunction. According to Whitehead, the experience of the combination of width and narrowness provides an "intensity of feeling"[14] or "zest."[15] And this corresponds to what we have called the experience of tension. Whitehead described the failure of aesthetic experience in the way we have described the failure of tension. Whitehead calls these failures "triviality" and "vagueness": "Thus 'triviality' arises from excess of incompatible differentiation. On the other hand, 'vagueness' is due to excess of identification."[16] Triviality is the loss of aesthetic value when remoteness overwhelms tension, and vagueness is the loss of value when closeness overwhelms tension. Finally, Whitehead indicates that the ideal aesthetic harmony has been attained when just that extreme of width has been reached where the addition of any further width would make the related factors become irrelevant to each other; consequently, progress requires that the course of history "must venture along the border of chaos."[17]

Charles Hartshorne, another "process philosopher," has virtually an identical description of aesthetic value:

> In fact, there is no case of harmony that is a clear exception to the principle of likeness in difference, similarity in the midst of contrast.
>
> If this principle is sound, there are only two ways of failing to achieve harmony—by too little contrast ("insipidity," "monotony"), and too little similarity ("discord," "incoherence," and "chaos").[18]

For Whitehead and Hartshorne, however, the aesthetic contrast is embodied only in the private and individual life of the observer. For example, Whitehead will say it lies in the subjective contrast between one's innovative interpretation of some reality (Appearance) and reality as it has been bluntly received from the past (Reality).[19] The theories of both men are organized around individuality, causality, and temporality. Neither of them can talk of the embodiment of aesthetic contrast in love or other social, noncausal, or nontemporal realities.

There is another pair of twentieth-century theorists who not only call for diversity within conjunction but relate this aesthetic definition to social situations. John Dewey and Morse Peckham each develop an aesthetic by reference to environments, and each attributes aesthetic value to a social circumstance: the social relation between an organism and its environment.

Dewey chooses to set aesthetic experience within what he calls normal experience; and normal experience refers, finally, to the social relation between an organism and its environment. "The first great consideration is that life goes on in an environment: not merely *in* it but because of it, through interaction with it. No creature lives merely under its skin."[20] For Dewey this interaction has two phases: "Life itself consists of phases in which the organism falls out of step with the march of surrounding things and then recovers unison with it—either through effort or by some happy chance."[21] He argues that the roots of aesthetic experience lie in one phase of this two-phase movement, the phase from the state of disruption with the environment to unison with the environment. The movement to new unison is similar to Tillich's movement to reunion. The experience of that movement is an aesthetic satisfaction.

Dewey's argument is biological, in that it is rooted in the phenomena of how an organism relates biologically to its environment. But Dewey extends his argument to refer, as well, to how the artist will intentionally cultivate occasions of discord, so as to heighten the ensuing consciousness of new harmonies. When, across the biological world, "participation comes after a phase of disruption and conflict, it bears within itself the germs of a consummation akin to the aesthetic."[22]

That movement is social and public; it lies in the "complete interpenetration of self and the world of objects and events."[23] But it also occasions experience that is private and individual. It can occasion aesthetic experience and provide a sense of "heightened vitality."

The movement from separation to unison requires that extremes, which might destroy that movement, be avoided. Dewey warns against problems comparable to the destruction of tension by either excess remoteness or excess closeness. Dewey says: "If the gap between organism and environment is too wide, the creature dies. If its activity is not enhanced by temporary alienation, it merely subsists."[24]

Morse Peckham, in *Man's Rage for Chaos: Biology, Behavior and the Arts,* is equally concerned with the aesthetic quality of the social relations between an organism and its environment. However, he finds aesthetic value in the other phase of the two-phase movement: while Dewey finds aesthetic value in the movement from remoteness from the environment to adjustment to the environment, Peckham concentrates on the movement from a dangerously close adjustment to the environment to a new diversity between the organism and its environment. Peckham explains the human tendency for disruption by reference to "man's rage for chaos." Dewey is concerned with how the organism might perish through falling too far out of touch with its changing environment, and he sees aesthetics as a comment on how the organism is restored to unison with its environment. Peckham is concerned with how the organism might perish through remaining so close to its present environment that it will be ill equipped for change when it does come. He sees aesthetics as a comment on how the organism disrupts its old ways of relating to the environment. In short, for Dewey aesthetics refers to the movement from separation to unison, while for Peckham it refers to the movement from unison to separation. Implicit in these notions of separation and unison is the idea that aesthetics has to do with diversity within conjunction.

Peckham's emphasis on the relation between aesthetics and overcoming excessive closeness between the organism and its environment comes as the result of looking at a puzzling situation. Why is it that people lavish the time, money, and energy they do on the arts, especially in a world that so much needs attention to human suffering? Peckham concludes "that the only way to approach the matter was to consider the artistic activity as a mode of biological adaptation."[25] Artistic activity and perception serve a particular role in biological adaptation; and they have to do with breaking old orders of adaptation to the environment.

The primary human drive is for order in the relations between the human and its environment. Any particular scheme of order is reached, in part, by ignoring certain data and concentrating on other data in the human environment. At some later day, when that ignored data becomes important in the environment, but continues to be ignored, there will be trouble. Obsolescence or extinction may be the consequence. But if old orders are broken in time, extinction is averted. So Peckham says:

There must, it seems to me, be some known activity which serves to break up orientations, to weaken and frustrate the tyrannous drive to order, to prepare the individual to observe what the orientation tells him is irrelevant, but what very well may be highly relevant. That activity, I believe, is the activity of artistic perception.[26]

Peckham then proceeds to argue that, contrary to common assumption, the arts have functioned not to create order but to bring chaos to old orders. Stated positively, art permits us to rehearse in a safe context those new ways of doing things, those new and deviant orders, which will be needed in new environments in the future.[27] That is the function of art: to rehearse the movement from union to disruption, in order to prepare the organism for new forms of adaptation.

Peckham's and Dewey's theories suffer, however, from an unbalanced concentration on the utility of aesthetic experience; they say that aesthetic pursuits foster biological adjustment. Johan Huizinga complained about a similarly unbalanced concentration on the utility of play. Huizinga notes that all biological explanations of play have one thing in common: "They all start from the assumption that play must serve something which is *not* play, that it must have some kind of biological purpose."[28] Huizinga goes on to say:

They attack play direct [*sic*] with the quantitative methods of experimental science without first paying attention to its profoundly aesthetic quality. . . . This intensity of, and absorption in, play finds no explanation in biological analysis. Yet in this intensity, this absorption, this power of maddening, lies the very essence, the primordial quality of play.[29]

If Huizinga's protest is accepted, it is apparent that what is needed are theories of art which explain more than the biological utility of artistic expression, which get closer than Dewey or Peckham do to explaining the inherent attractiveness of aesthetic phenomena and experience.

Leonard Meyer, in *Emotion and Meaning in Music*, attempts to explain just that inherently attractive quality of music, and he does that by emphasizing the unison to separation phase, the phase Peckham emphasizes. One listens to music with certain expectations about what will transpire musically. But when what does transpire deviates from the expected, the customary and the normative progression of sounds, the listener reacts emotionally. The old and normative orders are broken, chaos is injected. In the social relatedness between the listener, with his or her expectations, and the performance, with its violation of those expectations, there is tension. This tension is experienced with emotion.[30]

Meyer shows how "musical experiences of suspense are very similar to those experienced in real life."[31] So it is not improper to transfer what he says about music to aesthetic experience in general, or even into a comment on love. Just as the deviation from order in music engenders an emotional reaction in the listener, the increase of diversity in love's conjunction enhances the tension of the love and the tension in the experience of the love.

John Cage is equally interested in breaking the old musical orders. In *A Year from Monday* he explains why he is losing interest in being a composer, "When you get right down to it, a composer is simply someone who tells other people what to do. I find this an unattractive way of getting things done."[32] Cage would rather "give up the desire to control sound, clear his mind of music, and set about discovering means to let sounds be themselves rather than vehicles for man-made theories or expressions of human sentiments."[33] According to Cage, such sounds, such chaotic deviations from preconcocted orders, are

> a purposeful purposelessness or a purposeless play. This play, however, is an affirmation of life—not an attempt to bring order out of chaos nor to suggest improvements in creation, but simply a way of waking up to the very life we're living, which is so excellent once one gets one's mind and one's desires out of its way and lets it act of its own accord.[34]

In less vivid terms it can be said that the experience of diversity is intrinsically valuable.

So whether with Dewey one concentrates on the evil of chaos and calls for an aesthetics of order or whether with Peckham and Meyer and Cage one concentrates on the evil of excess order and calls for an aesthetics of chaos, one is still working with an aesthetics of diversity within conjunction.

One large question remains to be answered in these lectures.

What if the wise, who were so pessimistic about aesthetic love, were to break their vow of silence and to speak briefly? What if they were to refrain briefly from implying by their silence that aesthetic love is a bore? What if for a moment they were to stop being mum? What would they say?

Clearly, they would say that their talk about love was

only temporary. They would say that they were going to speak only long enough to ask, "What makes you think it's possible?"

After that the wise would resume their vows.

But even in that brief utterance the wise would reveal their wisdom. They would know that their question is distinctive. It does not mean what the skeptics would have meant if, during the last lecture, they had asked, "What makes you think it's possible?" The skeptics' question would have been a quantitative question. Having reached that point where they were willing to entertain metaphysical questions, and having heard us claim that aesthetic love can overcome solitude, the skeptics would have wanted to know whether there was the capacity to overcome solitude. The skeptic knows that very often people do not have in themselves the capacity to create a love among themselves. So the skeptics are concerned about a quantitative matter. Our argument met such questions by saying that aesthetic love's bondedness was synergistic, it included a greater quantity of bondedness than could be accounted for by looking at the sum of the capacities for bondedness held by those who were bonded. In short, we said that something more must have contributed to that bondedness.

But the wise, if they ask whether aesthetic love is possible, refer to quality, rather than quantity, and to aesthetics, rather than metaphysics. The wise are not asking about solitude, which is finally a question about quantity. The wise are asking about boredom, and that is a question about the absence of the quality of interest. So if the wise ask their question, they are really asking, What makes you think it's possible to create sufficient tension in the relationship to make me interested?

And this question reveals the wisdom of the wise. In the last analysis it is a question about innovation, and that is a difficult question, and the wise know that it is. What the wise really want to know is the quality of the relationship among diverse people. The wise have accepted our answer to the skeptics: that diverse people can be brought together. The wise want to know how they relate, once they are brought together. First, how can diverse people come to interact meaningfully? What do they do together? What do they say to each other? The question is, What quality of relatedness will permit interaction, once they are brought together? How, for example, do enemies relate to each other, once they are brought together? A new quality of relatedness is needed, but the enemies themselves do not seem capable of supplying it. What then is its source? Equally, in the opposite case, where closeness has overwhelmed tension, where people are involved in a cloying and monotonous relationship, how is it conceivable that diversity will be accentuated? The main problem with a monotonous marriage is that the possibilities for diversity are not appreciated. How then can those same spouses be expected to simply introduce forms of relatedness that will recognize or enhance a diversity between them? Again, an innovative quality of relatedness is needed, but the source of that innovation is not apparent.

The wise may be aware that any approach to innovation that confines itself to the closed system of the secular world—humans and their natural environment—is incapable of explaining the source of innovation. How could something really new, something that adds to the settled past, come itself out of that same settled past? How could something new, which adds to present people and their relations something that is not already in those people and their present relations, come itself out of those same people and their relations? Any effort to call the secular past or present the source of innovation is comparable to claiming that one can gain nourishment by eating out of one's own stomach.

The question of innovation is embarrassing, and the wise may know that. Morse Peckham notes that the behaviorists in the 1930's were embarrassed because they recognized that between the stimulus and the response something happened which made the response different from what, at the physiological level, the stimulus said the response should be. Peckham says that the behaviorists, to preserve their mechanical model, then introduced the notion of an "intervening variable."[35] Peckham then turns to aestheticians, who seem to have an equally difficult time of explaining the innovative element in art. Peckham belittles humanists who attempt to explain this element by calling it "creativity." He says that " 'creative' gives one such a warm and expansive feeling that it seems impossible that it is but a name for what it purports to describe and explain."[36] Peckham is contemptuous of the trickery in this designation. He says the humanists are hiding their ignorance from themselves and from us. To explain innovation by referring to human creativity is like saying, " 'The history of art is dynamic because the history of art is dynamic.' "[37] But, surely, Peckham should scrutinize his own terminology too. For his own "rage for chaos" seems equally to be only a name for what it purports to describe and explain. Certainly, Peckham goes on to explain the biological utility of the human rage for chaos; but that is not to explain its origin. Peckham, no more than the humanists, explains what it is which enables the introduction of new possibilities.

The question of innovation is a question the arts must always be asking. It is unlikely that they will find an answer through reference to the sciences; the sciences are primarily quantitative inquiries, useful for answering the skeptics' question, but not the question of the wise. But the arts seek the source of new qualities of relatedness. The arts specialize in innovation. But what is it which enables the artist to innovate? Does the artist, like God, create *de novo?*

What can be said to the wise but that the aesthetic quality of aesthetic love is made possible by some external source, that the innovative additions to the relations originate from outside the persons related? Perhaps that suggestion is no less embarrassing than the suggestions made by the behaviorists or the humanists, but it is a suggestion which is in accord with much philosophy, from Plato to Whitehead. Those philosophers have said that what we thought was invention is really discovery —that we do not originate realities but come upon actual or potential realities. And they have added that what we thought was discovery is really a guided tour —that we do not come upon those realities by ourselves, but are lured to them. They have agreed that something external functions to lure us mortals into innovative avenues. Whether this lure is called God may be a matter of indifference.

If it is called God (and we prefer to call it God), it is an estimate of God in a creative role. In the history of theology, when God innovates or fosters innovation,

God is said to function in a creative capacity, rather than in a redeeming capacity. This is God functioning as God would function before the fall, to encourage the positive presence of something intrinsically valuable. God confronts the void of aesthetic value and suggests that the void be filled with something positive. The void is indicated by the phenomenon of boredom and the void is filled when boredom is replaced with interest. The God of aesthetic love lures people involved in relations devoid of tension to entertain innovations, innovations which will overcome the problems of excessive remoteness and excessive closeness. The human capacity to receive and incorporate these innovations in practice may be called creativity or, alternatively, the rage for chaos and the rage for order.

The God of *agape* and *eros* is not the Creator God[38] but the Redeemer God. The God of *agape* and *eros* operates after the fall, attempting to redeem humanity from its failure.

The God of aesthetic love is God working to overcome sins of omission by fostering a positive love, a love that will deal with the failure of interest in love. The God of *agape* and *eros* is God working to overcome sins of commission, by fostering a love that will overcome past acts of destruction. The God of aesthetic love attempts to light fires in cold hearths. The God of *agape* and *eros* attempts to put out fires that never should have been lit. The God of aesthetic love, like a composer, seeks to innovate. The God of *agape* and *eros*, like a conductor, encourages performers to stop making mistakes.

In fostering aesthetic love, God works within that mystical and synergistic atmosphere which we discussed in last night's lecture. But tonight we are indicating that God can contribute to overcoming boredom, as well as to overcoming solitude. We are aware, however, that we have not said exactly how God lures the lovers to innovate.

Despite our inability to say how God fosters innovation, we would argue that even to use God language is to send an important signal. It is a way of indicating that the system is open, that we believe there are resources for love and aesthetic value which can invade what would otherwise be the closed system of ourselves and our environment. It is a way of saying that those mechanical models of the world, those models which feed only on mundane data, will be transcended. It is a way of saying that there is a creative addendum to what might seem to be the confines of our present prospects. And when the use of God-language signals this, it signals also that aesthetic love is not a secular love but a religious love.

The writers of Acts witnessed what happened at Pentecost, and they reverted to a theistic explanation. People so diverse that they could not speak the same language were brought together in such a way that each understood the other. Natural explanations seemed inadequate, so critics accused the people of being drunk on new wine. The writers of Acts relied on another explanation: this innovative conjunction of diverse people should be attributed to the workings of the Holy Spirit, which was among the people "like the rush of a mighty wind."

While we would read this story metaphorically, rather than literally, we would agree that some such explanation is needed. Is it sufficient to credit the warriors alone, when they meet one night between the trenches and tell stories? Is it sufficient to credit the tired workers alone, when their old conversation is suddenly animated?

We are proposing that it is not sufficient, that the innovative addition to a relatedness is attributable to an external source, to something more. And we are claiming that the aesthetic love which results is sufficiently satisfying to overcome the boredom of the wise.

But aesthetic love may be more than that. It may be more than just an expression of the good life. It may be more than just a love before the fall. It may be sufficiently satisfying to be a reason for getting out of bed in the morning. It may be sufficiently beautiful to be a reason for living after the fall.

YOUNG SEMINARIAN: One last question.

SPEAKER: Why not.

YOUNG SEMINARIAN: I don't know if I should ask this question.

SPEAKER: Don't worry.

YOUNG SEMINARIAN: But it is a question you still seem to be asking yourself.

SPEAKER: Then, surely, it is a question you can safely ask me.

YOUNG SEMINARIAN: I am a little bothered by your references toward God.

SPEAKER: What about them?

YOUNG SEMINARIAN: Can you tell me, in some other way, why you use the word "God"?

SPEAKER: Because I'm working that side of the street.

YOUNG SEMINARIAN: What street is that?

SPEAKER: Oh, let me tell it! The boulevard of explanation!

YOUNG SEMINARIAN: Boulevard?

SPEAKER: Alley.

YOUNG SEMINARIAN: Why don't you work the other side of the street? The side where the word "God" is not used?

SPEAKER: Why indeed.

YOUNG SEMINARIAN: Yes, why?

SPEAKER: For the gate is narrow and the way is hard.

YOUNG SEMINARIAN: And how is that?

SPEAKER: On that side of the street one must attempt to provide an exhaustive explanation, solely by reference to natural causes—that is, by reference to people, to nature, and to their concourse.

YOUNG SEMINARIAN: And what's wrong with that?

SPEAKER: Too hard.

YOUNG SEMINARIAN: But that's not the point. The point is, can it be done?

SPEAKER: Don't know.

YOUNG SEMINARIAN: So you will introduce the word "God" because it's easier that way?

SPEAKER: Easier.

YOUNG SEMINARIAN: But what about the growing body of literature providing an empirical explanation of love?

SPEAKER: Take a look.[39]

YOUNG SEMINARIAN: But what do they leave out?

SPEAKER: Something more.

YOUNG SEMINARIAN: Something more?

SPEAKER: Yes, something more.

YOUNG SEMINARIAN: Do you mean that you have included "God" merely because that word is a way of implying that there is . . .

SPEAKER: Yes, something more.

YOUNG SEMINARIAN: Is that all?

SPEAKER: Do you have to ask, Is that all? I said at the outset that I wanted to define and explain a phenomenon which has not been adequately defined and explained. How else could I have adequately explained the synergistic and innovative character of aesthetic love—except by acknowledging that there was something more?

YOUNG SEMINARIAN: Do you have to keep saying your "something more"?

SPEAKER: Besides, and finally, if the aesthetic value of love were appreciated, if aesthetic love were, in fact, seen to be our love before the fall, our taste of Eden, our glimpse of paradise, then we might from time to time be contented, even if there is . . .

YOUNG SEMINARIAN: . . . nothing more. This is getting easy.

SPEAKER: Young woman. Would you find it possible to make your way through all these empty chairs, to come up here for a little shaking of the hands?

YOUNG SEMINARIAN: Why not.

NOTES

Chapter I. Common Sense and Aesthetic Love

1. Plato, *Phaedrus*, tr. by R. Hackforth, in *The Collected Dialogues of Plato*, ed. by Edith Hamilton and Huntington Cairns (Bollingen Foundation, 1966), p. 495.

2. Statistics are from Robert Morgenthaler, *Statistik des Neutestamentlichen Wortschatzes* (Zurich: Gotthelf Verlag, 1958), pp. 67, 153, as cited in Victor Paul Furnish, *The Love Command in the New Testament* (Abingdon Press, 1972), pp. 220, 223.

3. Plato, *Phaedrus, Dialogues*, p. 497.

4. *Ibid.*, pp. 499–500.

5. Plato, *Symposium*, tr. by Michael Joyce, *Dialogues*, pp. 560, 562.

6. *Ibid.*, p. 553.

7. Nygren himself will acknowledge the validity of this claim. See Anders Nygren, *Agape and Eros*, tr. by Philip S. Watson (Harper & Row, Publishers, Inc., Harper Torchbooks, 1953), p. xiii. For a thorough discussion of the issues in the theological struggles to define *agape* from 1930 to 1972, see Gene Outka, *Agape: An Ethical Analysis* (Yale University Press, 1972).

8. Henry Miller, *The Rosy Crucifixion*, Book I, *Sexus* (Grove Press, Inc., 1965), pp. 26–28, 160–161, 269–270.

9. Harry Harlow, *Learning to Love* (Albion Publishing Co., 1973), pp. 8, 24, 35, 63.

10. Causality is a notion whose validity has been hotly disputed in philosophy since the time of David Hume. In contemporary physics, causality, if causality implies predictability, is of limited importance in describing the actions of particular particles. However, even if, with Hume, we termed causality a subjective rather than an objective phenomenon, it is significant as a way of describing our perceptions of love. And even if causality has limits as a way of describing the actions of particular particles, it remains adequate as a way of describing the gross actions of beings as large as humans.

11. See William D. Dean, *Coming To: A Theology of Beauty* (The Westminster Press, 1972), pp. 74–79.

12. We have followed here Rudolf Bultmann's interpretation, especially as that is presented in *Jesus and the Word*, tr. by Louise Pettibone Smith and Erminie Huntress Lantero (Charles Scribner's Sons, 1958).

13. Plato, *Theaetetus*, tr. by F. M. Cornford, *Dialogues*, p. 855.

14. Plato, *Symposium, ibid.*, p. 553.

15. Plato, *Phaedrus, ibid.*, pp. 499–501.

16. See Book VII of Plato's *The Republic*.

17. Such a pedagogy provides, by the way, a rationale for education of the elderly and fills what otherwise is a gap in pedagogy—that is, the gap between the apparent good sense in the education of elderly persons, who may never "use" that education, and a utilitarian pedagogy which demands that education be useful.

18. For example, The Institute of Personality Assessment and Research at the University of California at Berkeley has concentrated its study on highly creative individuals and the nature of the creative process. Don-

ald MacKinnon, said, while director of that institute: "The truly creative person is not satisfied with the solutions to his problems unless they are also aesthetically pleasing, unless, to use the mathematicians' term, they are elegant. The aesthetic viewpoint permeates all of the work of the creative person, and it should find expression in the teaching of all skills, and disciplines, and professions if creativity is to be nurtured." Donald W. MacKinnon, "Creativity: A Multi-faceted Phenomenon," *Creativity,* ed. by John Roslansky (Amsterdam: North Holland Publishing Company, 1970), p. 31.

19. Alfred North Whitehead, *Process and Reality* (Harper & Brothers, 1960), p. 25.

20. Time, after all, is expressed by reference to clocks, and clocks measure the displacement of something or, in the case of radioactive decay clocks, the dispersement of something, namely, the parts of an atom.

Chapter II. Western Theology and Aesthetic Love

1. See Mary Hesse, *Forces and Fields* (Littlefield, Adams & Co., 1961). Most efforts to describe natural processes are based on analogies that assume the reality of causality and, consequently, temporality (or, the chronological display of the entities causally related) and individuality (or, the separation from each other of the causal entities). The greatest difference between ancient and more modern (seventeenth to nineteenth century) analogies is that, while there is one basic modern analogy (the mechanistic analogy), there were many ancient analogies. The mechanistic analogy obviously presupposes causality, but the ancient analogies also presuppose causality. The latter simply say that "things may act upon one another to produce change and movement in many different ways." (*Ibid.,* p. 30.)

2. See Reinhold Niebuhr, *The Nature and Destiny of Man,* Vol. II (Charles Scribner's Sons, 1943), Ch. 3.

3. Daniel Day Williams, *The Spirit and the Forms of Love* (Harper & Row, Publishers, Inc., 1968), p. 136.

4. See *ibid.,* pp. 118–120.

5. *Ibid.,* p. 279. However, Williams distinguishes himself from the Augustinian tradition in important respects. Williams rejects the aseity (the ontological independence) of God, which permits God to act or to transform others, but not to suffer or to be transformed by others' actions; and Williams argues for the ontological dependence, as well as the ontological independence of God, which permits God to suffer action as well as to give action.

6. This is an interpretation of the Augustinian tradition which disagrees with Anders Nygren's unexplained assertion that Augustine's *caritas* is "not merely the sum" of *agape* and *eros,* "but forms a new, independent unity." (Nygren, *Agape and Eros,* p. 452.)

7. M. C. D'Arcy, *The Mind and the Heart of Love* (Meridian Books, Inc., 1960), p. 83.

8. *Ibid.,* pp. 300–301.

9. John Macmurray, another exponent of mutual love, in *Persons in Relation* (Harper & Brothers, 1961), describes ideal human relations in a way that appears to conform to aesthetic love. His notion seems to resemble Martin Buber's I-You relation, which is similar to aesthetic love. Macmurray will say, "Formally stated, 'I' is one term in the relation 'You and I' which constitutes both 'I and You.' " (P. 28.) However, it becomes clear that this relatedness is actually a version of *agape;* Macmurray's concern is that the self care for the other rather than that the self be interested in the relation between the self and the other (see p. 158).

10. D. T. Suzuki, *Mysticism, Christian and Buddhist*

(Harper & Row, Publishers, Inc., 1971), p. 6.

11. Georgia Harkness, *Mysticism: Its Meaning and Message* (Abingdon Press, 1973), p. 23.

12. Martin Buber, *I and Thou*, tr. by Walter Kaufmann (Charles Scribner's Sons, 1970), pp. 54–55.

13. *Ibid.*, p. 66.

14. *Ibid.*, p. 123.

15. *Ibid.*, p. 89.

16. Nygren, *Agape and Eros*, p. 735; see also p. 129.

17. *Ibid.*

18. It could be argued that *agape* and *eros* are forms of I-It relationships. *Agape* and *eros* share with the I-It relationship the characteristics of causality, temporal separation of the self and the other, and the consequent separation of individuals from each other. This is said in full knowledge of the fact that *agape* is frequently described and defended as a form of I-Thou, or I-You, relationship.

19. Buber, *I and Thou*, p. 100.

20. *Ibid.*, pp. 62–63.

21. *Ibid.*, pp. 93–94.

22. *Ibid.*, p. 63.

23. *Ibid.*, pp. 54, 56, 60.

24. *Ibid.*, p. 60.

25. Martin Buber, *Hasidism and Modern Man*, tr. by M. Friedman (Harper & Row, Publishers, Inc., Harper Torchbooks, 1966), p. 40.

26. *Ibid.*, p. 69.

27. For example, see Harkness, *Mysticism: Its Meaning and Message*, pp. 66, 70, 130.

28. Paul Tillich, *Systematic Theology*, Vol. III (The University of Chicago Press, 1963), p. 143.

29. For an example of such a tripartite analysis of Tillich's God, see William D. Dean, "The Universal and the Particular in the Theology of Paul Tillich," *Encoun-*

ter, Vol. 32, No. 4 (Autumn 1971), pp. 278–285.

30. Tillich, *Systematic Theology,* Vol. III, p. 129.

31. *Ibid.,* p. 112.

32. Paul Tillich, *Dynamics of Faith* (Harper & Brothers, Harper Torchbooks, 1958), p. 113.

33. Paul Tillich, *Love, Power, and Justice* (Oxford University Press, 1960), p. 25.

34. Before we leave this discussion of Tillich, it should be acknowledged that Tillich does use the term *agape.* But his use of the term has little similarity to the use of the term in these lectures. These lectures have accepted the popular dichotomy between *agape* and *eros.* Tillich disagrees with this dichotomy, saying that an "attempt has been made to establish an absolute contrast between *agape* and *eros.* " (Tillich, *Systematic Theology,* Vol. III, p. 137.) *Agape* for Tillich is "an ecstatic manifestation of the Spiritual Presence . . . the state of being drawn into the transcendent unity of unambiguous life." *(Ibid.) Agape* for Tillich is similar to aesthetic love; rather than a giving by one being to meet the needs of another, it is a participation in that mystical efficacy of the Spiritual Presence which makes love between humans possible.

35. Tillich, *Systematic Theology,* Vol. III, p. 134.

36. Buber, *I and Thou,* p. 123.

37. Erich Fromm, *The Art of Loving* (Harper & Brothers, 1956), p. 9.

38. *Ibid.,* pp. 18–20.

39. *Ibid.,* p. 80.

Chapter III. Ethics and Aesthetic Love

1. William and Paul Paddock, *Famine—1975! America's Decision: Who Will Survive?* (Little, Brown & Company, 1967), p. 51.

2. For example, see Garrett Hardin, "Lifeboat Ethics: The Case Against Helping the Poor," *Psychology Today*, September 1974, pp. 38 ff., or Garrett Hardin, "Living on a Lifeboat," *Bioscience*, Vol. 24, No. 10 (October 1974), pp. 563–568.

3. See, for example, William and Elizabeth Paddock, *We Don't Know How: An Independent Audit of What They Call Success in Foreign Assistance* (Iowa State University Press, 1973).

Chapter IV. Solitude and Aesthetic Love

1. Ernest Hemingway, "A Clean, Well-lighted Place," *The Snows of Kilimanjaro and Other Stories* (Charles Scribner's Sons, 1961), p. 32. Used by permission.

2. Erich Fromm, *The Art of Loving*, p. 8.

3. *Ibid.*

4. Edward Albee, *A Delicate Balance* (Pocket Books, 1970), pp. 54–56; stage directions omitted.

5. One could well ask the skeptic, even at this point, whether such a void is, finally, simply an alternative metaphysical foundation. Everett W. Hall, in *Philosophical Systems: A Categorical Analysis* (The University of Chicago Press, 1960), argues that implicit in all philosophical systems, even systems ostensibly skeptical about metaphysics, there are categorical commitments (p. 41), and that categorical commitments are metaphysical assumptions (p. 4).

6. Nygren, *Agape and Eros*, p. 216; see also *ibid.*, pp. 75 and 212.

7. Buber, *I and Thou*, p. 158.

8. Tillich, *Systematic Theology*, Vol. III, p. 129.

9. See Hesse, *Forces and Fields*, pp. 275–279. In an alternative interpretation, the exchange particle is seen

as merely an extended form of causality, with the exchange particle functioning as a causal agent for the related entities. This would see the relationship between the nuclear particles as a causal relationship and would not permit an analogy between the field of force and aesthetic love.

10. Whitehead, *Process and Reality*, p. 317.

11. *Ibid.*, p. 33.

12. *Ibid.*, pp. 326–327.

13. *Ibid.*, p. 320.

14. *Ibid.*, p. 95.

15. It could be argued that I have committed the fallacy of simple location; that is, I have said a person, for example, is *"here* in space and *here* in time, or *here* in space-time, in a perfectly definite sense which does not require for its explanation any reference to other regions of space-time" (Alfred North Whitehead, *Science and the Modern World* [The New American Library of World Literature, Inc., 1962], p. 50). In other words, it could be argued that I have artificially restricted what I have meant by an entity, and thereby ignored the actual social ties which that entity has with its contemporaries. I would reject this argument, however, on the grounds that simple location is a problem primarily because it neglects the "reference to any other times, past or future" (*ibid.*, p. 52); it is this restriction which isolates the entity from other spaces, in the past or future. The fallacy, in other words, refers primarily to a restriction in time, rather than to a restriction in the present space. I am referring to the spatial restriction. I have sought to discuss the spatial restriction of the present actual entity in the present actual world.

16. Whitehead, *Process and Reality*, p. 254.

17. *Ibid.*, p. 37.

18. David L. Hall, in *The Civilization of Experience: A Whiteheadian Theory of Culture* (Fordham Uni-

versity Press, 1973), has provided an excellent Whiteheadian theory of culture. But in doing so he has adopted Whitehead's own notions of process and causality. As a consequence, he has failed, I believe, to show how the social entity, which a culture must be, can be known as a present phenomenon.

19. Finally, we are aware that for certain audiences any comment on Whitehead requires book-length documentation. And we are aware that these few comments on Whitehead will fail to satisfy such audiences. But one brief word on one problem may be due any audience familiar with Whitehead. We have spoken as though a human being is an actual occasion, that smallest quantum of experience, whereas this is technically false. In fact, for Whitehead a human being is a society of actual occasions (sharing certain characteristics) with a personal (enduring) order. In other words, a person is a coherent agglomeration of occasions of experience with a certain continuity through time.

However, what we have said can be legitimately applied to persons. Even Whitehead, in books such as *Adventures of Ideas,* readily applies notions developed by reference to atomic occasions to the experiences of persons. Also, given Whitehead's system, a person does not have a sufficiently enduring personal order through time to permit past information to serve as present information about literal contemporaries, the way substance philosophy might. A person still is in process and is a somewhat new society with a somewhat new personal order each moment.

Chapter V. Boredom and Aesthetic Love

1. Johan Huizinga, *Homo Ludens: A Study of the Play Element in Culture* (Beacon Press, Inc., 1970), p. 11.

2. Albert Camus, *The Myth of Sisyphus*, tr. by Justin O'Brien (Random House, Inc., Vintage Books, 1955), p. 91.

3. George Santayana, in *The Sense of Beauty: Being the Outline of Aesthetic Theory* (Dover Publications, Inc., 1955), is in agreement with this assessment when he places moral and aesthetic values in a means-end relationship.

4. See Paul Tillich, *A History of Christian Thought*, ed. by Carl E. Braaten, 2d ed., revised (Harper & Row, Publishers, Inc., 1968), p. 33.

5. F. David Martin, *Art and the Religious Experience: The "Language" of the Sacred* (Bucknell University Press, 1972), pp. 62–63.

6. *Ibid.*, p. 63.

7. Tillich, *Love, Power and Justice*, p. 27.

8. *Ibid.*, p. 25. It should be noted, however, that here Tillich is not referring to some aesthetic tension created by the overcoming of separation, but to the power utilized in that act of love. We would argue that the manifestation of love's power is aesthetically interesting.

9. Denis de Rougemont, *Love in the Western World*, tr. by Montgomery Belgion, revised ed. (Doubleday & Company, Inc., Anchor Books, 1957), p. 45. Of course, de Rougemont is opposed to such "love for its own sake."

10. *Ibid.*, p. 27.

11. Whitehead, *Process and Reality*, p. 427.

12. *Ibid.*, p. 426.

13. *Ibid.*, p. 170.

14. Alfred North Whitehead, *Adventures of Ideas* (The Free Press, 1967), p. 252.

15. *Ibid.*, p. 258.

16. Whitehead, *Process and Reality*, p. 170.

17. *Ibid.*, p. 169.

18. Charles Hartshorne, *Reality as Social Process* (The Free Press, 1953), p. 46.

19. Whitehead, *Adventures of Ideas*, p. 258.

20. John Dewey, *Art as Experience* (Capricorn Books, 1958), p. 13.

21. *Ibid.*, p. 14.

22. *Ibid.*, p. 15.

23. *Ibid.*, p. 19.

24. *Ibid.*, p. 14.

25. Morse Peckham, *Man's Rage for Chaos: Biology, Behavior and the Arts* (Schocken Books, Inc., 1969), p. x.

26. *Ibid.*, p. xi.

27. See *ibid.*, p. 314.

28. Huizinga, *Homo Ludens*, p. 2.

29. *Ibid.*, pp. 2–3.

30. See Leonard Meyer, *Emotion and Meaning in Music* (The University of Chicago Press, 1956), p. 32. It should be acknowledged, however, that Meyer, while not very concerned about the biological utility of art, does say that art, to be valuable, must have a consequence. He says that the emotional reaction to tension "is aesthetically valueless unless it is followed by a release which is understandable in the given context." (p. 28).

31. *Ibid.*

32. John Cage, *A Year from Monday* (Wesleyan University Press, 1969), p. ix.

33. John Cage, *Silence* (The MIT Press, 1971), p. 10.

34. *Ibid.*, p. 12.

35. Peckham, *Man's Rage for Chaos*, p. 308.

36. *Ibid.*, p. 310.

37. *Ibid.*, pp. 309–310.

38. When Nygren in *Agape and Eros* (pp. 78 ff.) argues that God's *agape* for humanity is "creative," he

means creation only in a weak sense, where what was lost is recovered, not creation where something which has never been is made.

39. See, for example, *Theories of Attraction and Love,* ed. by Bernard I. Murstein (Springer Publishing Company, Inc., 1971).